SEASONS OF THE
Heart

SEASONS OF THE
Heart

The Story of How God Saw Me Through Despair, Loneliness,
and the Silent Suffering of Not Being Seen or Heard, to
Healing, Peace, Inner Joy, and Ultimately Victory

DARLENE TRAPPIER

LIFEWISE BOOKS

SEASONS OF THE

Heart

The Story of How God Saw Me Through Despair, Loneliness, and the Silent Suffering of Not Being Seen or Heard, to Healing, Peace, Inner Joy, and Ultimately Victory

DARLENE TRAPPIER

Published by:

 LIFEWISE BOOKS
PO BOX 1072
Pinehurst, TX 77362
LifeWiseBooks.com

To contact the author visit darlenebtrappier.com

Print - 978-1-958820-64-3
Ebook - 978-1-958820-65-0

DEDICATION

I dedicate this book to my husband, children, and family, who were and still are my motivation for writing this book. Without your love and support, I could not have done it. I love you all.

SPECIAL THANKS

A special thank you to Charity Bradshaw, who believed in me and encouraged me to complete this project after fifteen years of procrastination.

DISCLAIMER

This memoir is a truthful recollection of actual events in the author's life. To maintain privacy and anonymity, some names were changed.

CONTENTS

Chapter Nine

INTRODUCTION

It is 6: oo a.m., and my world is quiet except for the sound of the forced air coming in to heat the house up. *Well, I guess that quietness just ended, my neighbor just started up his car so he can warm it to go to work. Time to get up and start my day.* As I sit in my bathroom and gaze into the mirror, I can see the marks life has left on my face. As I rub my eyes, I wonder who that person is looking back at me. Her eyes are a bit tired-looking, her laugh lines are a bit deeper, and wrinkles and white hair have taken up permanent residence.

I sit here wondering how I managed to make it to this point with everything life has thrown at me. I stand up, and I say to myself, "It's because you're a fighter and a winner!"

Chapter One

INNOCENCE

SUMMER DAYS

The house we lived in was on Park Avenue in a small town in Champaign, Illinois. It was next to the candy store, at least that was what I called it. I loved going to that store because we could get a bag of candy, a big pickle, and a peppermint stick for five cents. On summer days, my momma would let us out to go play and give us a few pennies to buy candy. Sometimes, I would even be outside playing in just my underwear, but I did not care because I was having fun, and no one noticed or cared what I had on.

Since I was one of the youngest in the family, I always wore hand-me-downs from older sisters and even older brothers. I would wear boys' and girls' underwear because we were poor, and momma could not afford to buy all eight of us clothing. She would buy for the four oldest kids, and when they outgrew their clothes, she passed them down to the four younger ones.

Even though life seemed carefree it was anything but in those days. We always had plumbing issues. With eight kids, two adults, and only one bathroom, it was bound to happen more times than not. Whenever the toilet was clogged, we would go outside. We were so poor that we could not afford an outhouse, so the backyard became the outhouse. We would go over to the pre-dug hole in the backyard, pick the leaves my momma showed us to use, and do our business. After we finished, we used a shovel and covered it for the next person to use. This was what true county living could be like for poor people.

THE BAD MAN

I can still hear the sound of the bedsprings on the old mattress when someone gets up from lying on it. My brother and I always hid under it when momma was "entertaining," as she would call it. We would laugh quietly, and sometimes, if we stayed under there long enough, we would fall asleep. However, there was one day when I did not hear the springs moving but rather the rattling of a squeaky old wooden chair. My stepfather was sitting in it while facing the double glass doors with the curtains on them for privacy in momma's room.

I heard him call my name, so I went to see what he wanted. I was young and innocent when he asked me to stand beside this noisy old chair, so I did. I was trying to crawl over one of his legs, but I could not because I was too little. My tiny arms could barely reach over his leg, no matter how hard I tried. I remember what I was wearing—the most beautiful, dark blue, bouffant dress with white dots all over the bottom. It had a white ribbon wrapped around and tied up in the back, and the top was white with a round collar. I thought it was pretty.

After I got tired of trying to reach over him, he started patting me on the top of my head, then he patted me on my back, and finally, he patted me on my bottom. It wasn't long after that when I felt a lot of pain in my private place. I started crying, and when my stepfather heard me, he stopped what he was doing and tried to get me to be quiet. I did not know why he was touching me in such a way, but I knew I did not like it.

My stepfather raised hunting dogs, so to calm me down, he placed a puppy on the floor in front of me. When I saw the puppy, I stopped crying even though my privates were still a little sore. Even though I was young, I understood as best as I could not to go near him anymore. After I finished playing with the puppy, I went looking for my momma throughout the house, but I could not find her. I thought, *Where is my momma?*

From that day on, he was the bad man I stayed away from because he hurt me. The house was a big enough place for a child as small as I was to hide from him whenever I wanted to. I found a lot of places to hide whenever I felt scared of him or anything else.

I'M HUNGRY, MOMMA!

Growing up, hunger was a constant companion, especially when there were eight mouths to feed and no financial support from any of their fathers. Yes, my mother had eight children with seven fathers. When I was around five years old, I asked my mother where my daddy was. She said she put him out for eating the last of the cornflakes. When I think about it now, we must have been struggling really badly if cornflakes could break up a relationship.

One day, I went to Momma and said, "I'm hungry, Momma!"

She said, "Okay," and took us younger girls in our *Wizard of Oz*[1] dresses to watch and wait for the neighbor across the way to go to sleep. You see, we only had a large twenty-five-pound sack of flour and a tub of lard to eat, but they had a vegetable garden and chickens. She waited until the streetlights came on because it became easier to see in the alley. Momma finally said it was okay for us younger kids to go and pick the vegetables while the older ones went to gently and quietly shew a couple of chickens out of the coup.

Even though we were young, she made it a point to teach us as best as she could how to make it in this world. She told us nothing would come free or easy, and we had to do what we needed to do to survive. Momma was also a good cook and taught us girls how to cook from scratch as well.

After we got the vegetables and chickens, Momma grabbed one of them and swung its neck until it popped, and then took the other one and chopped its head off. We watched those chickens run around until they dropped.

After Momma killed those chickens, she had us kids wash the vegetables and told my sister, Donita, to start the stove. Back then, we had a stove that needed the pilot lit. That stove was older than dirt, even as old as time itself, but it got the job done for cooking and heating the house. On cold nights, we slept downstairs to stay warm with a large pot of water on the stove so the heat was moist and did not dry us out.

Well, let me tell you something; that night, when Donita went down to light the pilot, someone was not paying attention and turned the gas on. All I could see was smoke accompanied by the smell of burnt hair. I was scared! After I saw that Donita was okay (minus some hair and eyebrows), I fell on that hard wooden floor and laughed until my stomach hurt. Meanwhile, Momma yelled at whoever turned the gas on. Despite the incident, we had the best fried chicken and steamed vegetables that night.

Life was so simple in Champaign. With the smallness of the town, we were able to run around and play all day. Of course, we had to go inside when the streetlights came on though. One night, we were outside watching my stepfather gather the trash in the backyard. Out in the country where we lived, we burned our trash instead of having it picked up by a garbage service. After he put all the trash in a pile, he set it on fire.

Little did he know that a plastic bottle was thrown in also, and plastic should never be in the burn pile. Once the fire grew hot and high, we heard a loud pop, and the plastic from the bottle exploded, hitting my sister in the face. She screamed bloody murder. My momma ran over and took her inside. I could not see what she was doing, but after a while, my sister stopped crying.

The next time I saw my sister, she had a bandage on her face because Momma was good at bandaging. Besides, Momma said it cost money to go to the hospital, and we didn't have enough for that. So, I became my sister's nurse and helped her get better with popsicles and candy. Yes, candy can heal everything.

NEW SEASON

When I was seven years old, life took a different turn into a new season because Momma said we were going to move to California to be with Big Momma (my grandma). Many of Momma's sisters were already living in Los Angeles at the time. We were all excited about this new adventure, so we packed up the car and started the five-day drive there. Since my younger brother and I were the smallest, we had to sleep in the back window of the car. It was a long car that fit all of us in it. Despite the fit, we had to make lots of bathroom stops. I always tried to hold mine in for as long as I could because Momma would get tired of stopping.

We finally made it to California and got to see all those lights. We went from darkness to light, then darkness all in one day. Seeing the lights meant we could finally stop and go to the bathroom, which was a huge relief for me! Once we got back in the car, we drove the rest of the way to Aunt Ida's house to stay for a while because Momma had to look for a place for us to live. My aunt's house was big and beautiful, and she even had a color television. I told my cousin Robbie, Ida's daughter, that I had never seen a color TV before. I thought they were rich because their house was big to me; they had a large kitchen with a pretty stove, a dining area, and a big backyard. We did not have any of that in Champaign.

One day, I woke up to Momma and Auntie arguing about the house being too small for so many people. We all slept on the floor in the living room, and my aunt said there was not enough room. Momma told Auntie that she had found us a house but needed another week to pay for it so we could move out, but Auntie did not want to hear it. Momma said we would move sooner, and Auntie did not have to worry about us anymore.

After that discussion, Momma went into the bedroom, and I could hear her crying. I went in and said, "Momma, why are you crying?" I tried to give her a hug, but she pushed me away and told me to go play outside. I was sad seeing my momma crying, and I did not like Auntie anymore because she caused it.

Harcourt Avenue was our new street until we grew up and moved out on our own. When we first drove to the house, we were all excited to go inside and see what it looked like. Momma showed us the boy's room and then the girl's room, which was at the back of the house. There was no furniture yet because we left everything in Champaign.

We slept on the floor for a while until Momma got us some furniture. I just treated it like a slumber party with my siblings. Momma bought bunk beds for us younger kids, and my oldest sister had her own bed.

Life in Los Angeles was exciting but also scary because things were larger, brighter, and louder than what I was used to in Champaign. However, I did love sitting in the front yard watching people go by so I could see who we were living around. After the incident with my stepfather, I was not a trusting person anymore, even at such a young age. Life can teach some beautiful and some ugly things. For me, I saw the ugly more than the beautiful from then on.

There was this one family that had all boys, and they came over to meet the new family, but they saw my older sisters and wanted to get to know them. As we got to know them, our families became like siblings, and I even considered them my new brothers. Their parents were nice, and Momma got to know them as well.

One day, I remember sitting in the front yard as I commonly did, and I asked God why I did not trust people and why I wanted to be a loner. You know what He said to me? I heard Him as plain as I heard my own voice. He said, "Trust me." I thought I was hearing things, but when I heard this, I became a little bit more relaxed. So, I kept on talking to Him every chance I got. Little did I know I was on my journey with Him and entering new seasons that would undoubtedly test my faith and strength.

EXPOSURE TO VIOLENCE

One day, when I was sitting in the front yard, I saw this horrific scene unfolding before my very eyes. The couple who lived across the street were arguing. The guy was angry with his girlfriend for some unknown reason to me, and he began to hit her with his fist. I was so scared that I did not move an inch because I thought that if he saw me, he would come beat me, too. While he was beating her, he dragged her over to the car and opened the trunk. I could not understand why he needed to do that. I eventually found out why.

He held onto her with one hand and took out a tire iron and began to beat her with it. She was screaming for her life, but no one came out of their house to help, and I could not understand why. My heart was feeling like it was going to jump out of my chest with every blow against her back. The sound was carried on the wind like a current. I slowly got up, crawled back to the house, and told my mother what was happening. She said to stay inside and mind my own business.

I thought this was a nice, clean neighborhood because the lawns were mowed nicely, palm trees lined the street, there was no trash anywhere, and it was quiet for the most part. But this day, I saw a different side—one I never thought I would see outside the closed door of our house with my mother and stepfather fighting.

I thought all the violence happened inside the house because that's all I knew. Ozell said, "Whatever happens in this house, stays in this house," and we all understood what would happen if it went outside. (Ozell is what Momma wanted us to call her because she said she would feel old if we called her Momma, so from now on, I will be addressing her as such.) No matter how bad it was, we never spoke about it until we were all adults.

That situation across the street reminded me of the reason my stepfather no longer lived with us. There was this one night when my mother stayed out all night, and my stepfather went to find her. Well, he did all right, and she was not where she said she would be. They started arguing before they made it home, but when they got inside the house, the violence began. They began fighting each other, and my stepfather got the sawed-off shotgun and began beating her in the face with the butt of it after he knocked her down to the floor. All of us kids were screaming and trying to get him off her, but he just pushed us aside so he could continue beating her.

While this was happening, my oldest brother, Gary, who was seventeen or eighteen at the time, was not home. He did not like our stepfather, so there was bad blood between them already. After he finished beating my mother, he got up, and I yelled, "I'm telling Gary when he gets home!" He then got up and left the house, and my mother went to the hospital to get herself checked out. The rest of us kids stayed home and cried because we did not know if she was coming back or if my stepfather, the monster, would come back before she did with his targets set on us.

Well, Gary came home before both of them, and we told him what had happened. He waited until Ozell came home and asked her what happened. She told him to leave it alone, and he said no. Gary was not happy, and this was the opportunity he was waiting for to get rid of the monster living in our house. Finally, our stepfather returned home, and Gary was waiting for him. Gary was younger and stronger, so Gary beat him up and threw him out of the house on his back. He landed in the driveway and left. Ozell finally realized the choice she had to make between the monster and us. If she had let him stay, it would not have been safe for him in the future because his life would have been put on the line since Gary had connections with the Crips gang and Mexican gangs.

This was when I started to stay to myself more. I did not know or understand that these feelings were anxiety, PTSD, and depression. I was talking with my younger brother, Albert, one day about how I was sick and tired of everything going on in the house, and we decided together to run away. We were only about eight and ten then, so we took a few clothes, put them in a trash bag, and left. We only got as far as the corner house that belonged to the lady that Ozell did not like and told her why we were running away. She said we could stay there, but little did we know, she called our mother and told her what was going on. Ozell told her to tell us to come home, and we would talk about it.

Child, that was the worst decision we ever made because as soon as we entered the yard, Ozell was waiting for us with an extension cord in her hand. She beat us mercilessly. I had bleeding welts all over my body, from my neck to my ankles. They were so bad that I could not wear pants or long sleeves for a couple of weeks. Everyone saw the marks on my body. She punished me more than Albert because he was the youngest and her favorite.

I was about ten then, and Albert was two years younger than me. He didn't get as many beatings as the rest of us, I think, because she loved his father so much that she could hardly bring herself to whip Albert. When it was time for all the younger kids to get a "whipping," as Ozell called it (I called it a beating), Albert would run and hide, so by the time she finished with us she was too tired to beat him.

FAMILY

In 1970, the Vietnam War was going on, and my oldest brother, Gary, enlisted in the Marines as a way out of the house. It broke my heart because I felt that I was losing my brother and father, protector, and best friend. When it was time to take him to the bus, I sat on his lap, cried all the way, and begged him not to leave. This was the beginning of the negative feelings I had toward Ozell because, to me, she was the reason he had to leave.

When we got to his drop-off, they had to peel me off him. I screamed for him not to leave me. As he got on the bus, he turned to me and said, "I'm coming back for you," then left. At that moment, I felt as if my world had just crumbled, and I wanted to die. I watched until I could not see the bus anymore and cried so much in the car that I fell asleep.

I counted every day he was gone. Finally, Gary's graduation from basic arrived. It was one of the best days of my life. I got up early, ate breakfast, got dressed, and waited outside to go see him after his absence for a long two months. We all loaded into Ozell's car and drove a couple of hours to Camp Pendleton for his military graduation.

He was so handsome in his black uniform, standing straight up in formation. I was so proud of Gary because he made it out and was doing something with his life. I really missed his big smile and the huge hugs he gave me. He taught me how to comb my hair, about personal hygiene, and how to handle my money, which I was not so good at then. I learned a lot from him. He was my brother, but he also acted like a dad. I guess since he was the oldest and I was the youngest girl in the family, he took special care of me, and I didn't mind it one bit.

Gary came home from the base on weekends and often brought friends with him. One time, they stole a military bus and brought a lot of guys to the house, and we celebrated the whole weekend. But when Sunday came, the realization that they would have to face punishment began to set in. They were all disciplined, and Gary was put in the military jail. He really did not like taking orders and stayed in trouble a lot until the military decided it was best to release him.

He was not the only hothead in the family; my oldest sister, Judy, was also a hand full for my mother. When we moved to Los Angeles, she had a hard time adjusting to the bright lights of this big city and all that it had to offer. She became a mother at fifteen, got involved with the wrong crowd, and started down the road of a lifetime battle with drug addiction. She had four boys and her youngest was a girl. I loved my oldest sister but always worried about her because we never knew where she was until she showed up at Ozell's door looking tired from being beaten down by the streets.

Judy was no punk, though; she could hold her own. She might have been small in stature but so is dynamite. That was my beautiful sister Judy, and she could sing like a songbird. When she passed away from a violent assault, my heart sank because I knew I would never hear her voice or get a hug from her again. She did leave behind four of her five beautiful children. One passed before her at the tender age of three. They all had some aspect of her personality, be it good or bad, but I still love them all to this day.

Next, there is my gentle spirited brother Bobbie, who is special needs. He has the mind of a five-year-old but a heart of gold. Ironically, out of my four oldest siblings, he was the only one to graduate high school. Imagine that. He never gave us any problems, and after my mother passed away, he stayed at her house with my younger brother Albert until Donita came and moved him with her. We do not know exactly what happened in the house between him and Albert, but Bobbie hates him with a passion.

Then, there is my sister Rose, who I did not get along with, and it was not because I didn't try but because she was a few years older and was not into spending time with her younger siblings.

We never really established a relationship even though we were sisters. She had the prettiest legs, and she knew it because she always wore short skirts so she could show them off. Rose was the most self-centered of all us kids. I guess because she had lighter skin than most of us, and she was aware of it.

Back then, if you were of a lighter shade as a black person and had a better texture of hair, you were considered more attractive, so she took full advantage of her lightness, even though she wasn't that cute in the face. I could not understand how someone could be born into the same family yet treat them like strangers. When we lived in Champaign, we were very close to each other, but when we hit L.A., we could not have been farther apart even in the same house.

After living in L.A. for a couple of years, I became more of a loner and only trusted Donita and Gary. It seemed trouble was always coming to our doorstep, and I wondered if we would ever be a happy family again or was I the only one who thought we were happy in the first place.

My tender-hearted sister Linda, who was born with Down syndrome, was kind and had a beautiful spirit. I enjoyed being around her because she reminded me that there was still sweetness in the world. She had hips that made her sway when she walked, and at four feet and eleven inches, she wiggled a bit.

One night after we all went to bed, we were awakened by a loud thud, so I jumped up to see what was going on. It was my sister having a seizure so hard and loud it made her whole bed jump up and down. It scared the life out of me because I had never seen that before. Now, I understood why Ozell taped a spoon on the wall over her bed. Donita ran into Ozell's room and woke her up. Ozell rushed into our room, took the spoon, and put it in Linda's mouth to hold her tongue down, turned her on her side, and waited for it to end. After that, I was scared to be in the same room until I witnessed it several times, then it was nothing.

Chapter Two
FEAR

STRANGER DANGER

As time passed and we grew up, Gary and sisters Judy and Rose moved out on their own while I and my remaining siblings were finding where we fit in. It was time to enroll in school, so Ozell took us all to our schools so we could start on time for the new year. The older kids went either to Dorsey High School or Mount Vernon Junior High School, but the younger ones went to Virginia Road Elementary School. It was a nice school, and the kids were nice to us too.

When Momma went to enroll Donita and me, they told her we had to take a test to see how smart we were. I did so good I skipped a grade, but Donita didn't, and she was held back, which didn't upset me because now we were in the same grade and could spend so much time together, so I thought.

They ended up putting us in different classrooms down the hall from each other. I loved Donita because she was my hero and best friend. School was easy for me, and I enjoyed going to art class because of Mrs. Jones. She took time with me after school so I could listen to her explain how good I was doing. I enjoyed helping her and stayed so long that I would sometimes get left behind by my little brother and sister. The fourteen blocks to get home were short, so I didn't mind walking alone.

Until one day, I decided to stay after school to help my teacher again. Little did I know that day would turn dark. I helped Mrs. Jones as always and told Donita to go home, and I would catch up as soon as I was done helping. I left later than usual, and all the other kids in our neighborhood that we normally walked home with had left, so I was left to walk home alone. I wasn't scared because I had done it so many times before.

As I was on my way home, a tall white man stopped me and asked if I would try on some sandals that he had bought for his daughter, who was nine or ten years old like me, and said I looked like I wore the same size shoe. I sat down on the curb of the street, took off my shoes, and tried on the sandals. Something told me to look up at the man, and he was looking around for some reason. I felt nervous, so I took the sandals off, grabbed my shoes, and began to run all the way home. I didn't stop until I reached my house, and I didn't look back to see if he was following me either.

My heart was beating so fast that after I made it home and was trying to catch my breath, I knew if I told Momma, she would beat me. I remembered the little boy who went missing a few years prior, and I thought to myself, *Man, that could have been me.*

My mother was a strict woman and raised us the way she was raised. When we messed up or if she was angry for any reason, we got beat. Depending on how mad she was determined what we were beat with and for how long. We could have been beaten with a belt, extension cord, fist, tree branch, or a piece of a water hose, or she would threaten to get her gun. With that thought in my mind, I kept it to myself.

As an adult, it is strange to think I never told anyone about that. From that day on, I didn't stay after school to help anyone. I walked home with my sister, little brother, and the other kids from my neighborhood and kept a lookout for that man every day. On Friday, I was glad I didn't have to go to school the next day.

Saturday was my day to spend time soaking up sunlight in the front yard. I spent a lot of time there on a sheet with my snacks, watching people as they went about their daily lives. I guess I was the neighborhood watchman. *The sun feels good today,* I said to myself as I relaxed on the soft grass.

I always enjoyed my alone time because it gave me space to speak to God. Little did I know I was developing a relationship with Him as I sat out there for hours. There were times when I would spend so much time talking to Him about my week, and what I had been through that I would fall asleep and wake up just before the sun went down. It seems crazy to do that today, but back then life was much simpler, and we didn't have to worry about being kidnapped from our yard because someone was always sitting out on their porch or other kids were playing on the street. However, there were other monsters I had not yet seen that would eventually show themselves.

OZELL

I loved Ozell very much, but I always felt she didn't love me because she would beat us when she was angry, if she lost money during her poker games, or a relationship would end. I think this tendency was because she had a hard life growing up. She lived in rural Mississippi and started having children at thirteen. By the time she was twenty-six, she had eight children in addition to two abortions and three miscarriages. She raised us with a third-grade education and did the best she could. I was still proud of her being my mother. Besides, everyone said I looked the most like her.

Ozell was raised in a town called Edwards back in the 1930s. She was the tenth of twelve children and didn't know she had siblings until she was about ten years old. When she was eight, two of her young friends were severely raped, and that scared her tremendously. Afterward, she went to one of her dad's (my grandfather) friends and asked him to "open her up." The man said yes, but she had to pay him two dollars to do it.

So, according to some of my aunts, she did what she could to raise the money. She collected pennies, nickels, dimes, and quarters until she raised the two dollars and took it to my grandfather's friend. He took his time and did what they called back then opening her up. I asked why she did it, and I was told that she was afraid that what happened to her friends would happen to her. How could that be the mentality of an eight-year-old? It helped me to understand but not accept why Ozell was the way she was. She always had a hard outer exterior, but there were times when I could see a crack and catch a glimpse of her softer side. They were few and far between, but they were there.

When she was ten years old, her father told her she had a choice: either start paying rent or move out. I guess she chose to move out and deal with the world on her own. It was also around that time when she found out she had other siblings. I remember when the original movie *The Color Purple*[2] came out, and I was in her bedroom watching it when she saw the character Mister on the screen; she yelled to turn the channel. I asked her what was wrong, and she said nothing. Later, I found out from relatives that Mister was much like her father with a hate-filled personality. He was allegedly so mean that he had what they called a whipping post in the cellar and would strip my uncles and beat them with a cat of nine tales.

One day he came home from work and went toward his personal chair to sit down. Before he could, he had a massive heart attack and died right where he stood. Decades later, when my grandmother was on her deathbed (of which I was present), my aunt called my mother and told her to get over to her house. I jumped in the car with her, and we drove quickly to my Aunt Lee's house.

When we got there, my cousin held my grandmother in her arms and was about to lay her down when my grandmother said, "Don't lay me down," and my cousin sat her back up. As soon as she sat back up, my grandmother said, "Don't bury me next to that man." It was then all the horrible stories I had heard over the years became real to me. It's strange because that was the first time since moving to California that I saw my mother crying her heart out.

PLEASE BELIEVE ME

Ozell played poker a lot. Sometimes, they played at our house, and other times, she went elsewhere. My mother was addicted to gambling. She would stay away for days when she was winning and just overnight when losing. I loved interacting with the players and learning the game whenever she would have them at our house. I would say to myself, *Those poker games were a riot.* I remember when she started having them at the house. She cooked a buffet that I would serve to her guests. The food was only for them, and she would serve us either pork 'n beans, hot dogs, or chili every Friday, and I hated those meals for a long time after I grew up.

I asked her if I could help, and she said yes. I spent as much time with her as I could to show her, I wanted to be around her and hoped she loved having me there too. We would talk about what she was cooking, and she would show me how she made everything from scratch. I so enjoyed those times.

When it was time to prepare for her poker guests to arrive, I would sit in the living room and greet them, take their coats to hang up in the closet, and she had a lock box for their guns because it had to be safe for everyone there. I couldn't understand why they would bring guns into our house.

Ozell always had guns ever since she was younger, and we grew up with her having them in her bedroom. She had several guns: a .38-snub nose, a .357 Magnum, a sawed-off shotgun, and a .45. We never asked her why she had them, but we were always afraid of her because of them. She even slept with one under her pillow, so I made sure never to get into her bed, no matter what.

MR. S.

When I served her poker guests, they would tip me a dollar for a cup of coffee, and for a plate of food, I would get five dollars. I did this all night until around 1:00 a.m., when I went to bed. I got up at 6:00 a.m., took my shower, got dressed, and began cooking breakfast for them. You see, they would play poker for two to three days straight.

I began serving coffee and breakfast plates, and the tips would start all over again. By this time, I was fourteen years old, and I could see that the men she gambled with were starting to notice the physical changes I was going through. This made me feel very uncomfortable, but I never said anything to her. I made sure I always stayed away from where they were gambling in the house unless they ordered coffee or a plate of food.

One Saturday morning, when I got up as usual to go and take my shower, something happened. After I showered and got dressed, I opened the door "Mr. S." was waiting right outside. When our eyes met, I could see he had a not-so-nice look in his eyes. He shoved me back into the bathroom, closed the door, and began grabbing me all over. I was so scared that I didn't scream, but I kept trying to push him away. He said things like, "I have been watching you," and "I want to take care of you if you let me." I kept telling him, "No!" but he kept trying to put his hands inside my clothes. All I could think of was, *Where is Ozell?*

It wasn't until I said I was going to tell her that he stopped and left me alone in the bathroom. I was so scared that I almost peed on myself. I stayed in that bathroom for what seemed like forever, but I knew I had to come out because it was the only full bathroom in the house.

After I finally had the nerve to open the bathroom door, I heard a commotion coming from where they were playing poker. Mr. S got into an altercation with another man, and Ozell and the others tried to break it up. By this time, my sister had woken up because of the loud noise and came running into the kitchen, which was opposite the poker room. We both stood there watching all this happening.

When Mr. S saw me, he kept his eyes on me, and Ozell turned to see what he was looking at. She saw my eyes, which by now were full of fear, and she yelled out, "The poker game is over! Everyone needs to leave!" I grabbed my sister's hand and ran to the back of the house where our bedroom was and told her what happened. She asked me if I was going to tell Ozell, and I said I was scared too. She told me I had to tell her.

After the poker game ended and all the people left, Ozell went into her bedroom and closed the door. She said, "I don't want to be disturbed." So, I left it alone until she woke up the next day, which was Sunday. I knocked on her door and asked if I could come in. She said yes. I told her I wanted to talk to her about something, but at first, she didn't want to listen to me. I felt she knew what was up but didn't want it confirmed. I began to tell her what happened, thinking she would protect me, but instead, she blamed me for dressing a certain way.

I always wore long shirts and jeans when I served her poker guests, so I couldn't understand why she would blame me instead of Mr. S. She told me I needed to keep that situation to myself because she didn't want it to affect her poker games. From then on, I didn't serve her guests anymore.

I ran out of her bedroom with tears running down my face and told Donita what happened. She said, "Don't worry, I believe you, sister." She was my best friend and my protector in those days. Being a year older than me and since I was small for my age, she made sure no one would hurt me. Donita was always my safe space, my go-to person, my sister, my best friend. We even got pregnant just a few months apart after we were adults.

Donita took over once I stopped serving Ozell's poker games, but no one dared to come at her because they all thought she was a lesbian. It's funny when I think about it because she always wore overalls and had a scarf on her head. She would wash her hair, oil it, for some reason put rollers in it, and then put a scarf on but never took it off. One time, she left rollers in it for so long that her hair began to grow around the sponge rollers. Lord, why would she do that? I still laugh hard even thinking about that.

Donita and I never had an argument or disagreement in our entire lives. If she was ever mad at me, she never let me see or hear it. We were always there for each other. Whatever money I made from working Ozell's poker games, I shared with her and vice versa. I remember making two hundred dollars in just one weekend when school was about to start. I told Donita I would split the money with her so we could catch the bus to the mall and get school clothes. Ozell stopped buying us clothes when we got into high school, so Donita and I made sure we took care of each other while Ozell took care of our special needs brother and sister. The rest of us had to provide for ourselves.

GARY

My other best friend was my oldest brother Gary, who I call my "brother father." He was also my hero and the one who taught me about becoming a woman. I began my period late at the age of fourteen. When I woke up one morning to go to the bathroom and saw blood all over my pajamas, I got scared. I ran to Ozell's room and knocked on the door. She said I could come in, and I showed her my pajamas. She said, "Go look under the sink in the bathroom." I went, and all I found were these long, brown, thin boxes with a white pad-type thing and two safety pins.

I didn't know what to do, so I ran into the boy's bedroom and woke up Gary. He got up, took me back into the bathroom and walked me through what to do so I could finish getting dressed. Afterward, he taught me about how I was able to get pregnant if I had sex, but that was the furthest from my mind. I loved Gary with all my heart. He always had a smile that could melt butter with that silver tooth he had put in. But boy, when he got mad, he saw red, so I always tried to stay on his good side.

Gary was the oldest of the eight children, then there was my sister Judy, Bobbie, Rose, Linda, Donita, me, and the brat Albert, who was the youngest and quite spoiled. Gary took care of all the kids because Ozell was always out gambling or sleeping after three or four days of being away. She always left money for us before she left and a way to reach her if we needed to, but Gary was the one who made sure we were taken care of.

LINDA

My sister Linda, with Down syndrome, had a smile so genuine that when she smiled, it seemed to wash away all the darkness saturating my world. Losing her at the age of twenty to walking pneumonia stole a piece of my heart. I was five months pregnant with my first child when she passed away. I was sitting on the washer in the hallway when they put her in the body bag and wheeled her out of the house.

I remember when Linda would get mad if she caught you at the wrong time and in the wrong position. She'd punch you, and I guarantee you felt it. We all took turns taking care of her and Bobbie, who was also special needs. They were the most tender and genuine, loving people I ever had in my life. One time, one of my uncles came over and was playing with all of us kids while my mother was in the front of the house. We were at the back of the house wrestling with him when, after a while, we all got tired of playing and went outside.

After a while, Linda came outside with her hair all messed up. I asked her what happened to her hair, and she said, "Uncle E (as I'm going to call him) was touching me inside my clothes, and I kept trying to push him away until finally he let me go."

I ran inside and told Ozell what Linda said. She got her gun and went after my uncle, but by the time she reached him, he had already left the house because he knew he was in trouble for what he had done to Linda. After that, I never trusted or liked that man. To this day, I'm not very trusting because of the pain I endured as a child and as a young adult.

When a child goes through abuse in any form, it cripples them for a season. Their heart must heal, and that healing can only come from a loving God. As I look in the mirror, I can see the lines of history in my eyes staring back at me, and it reminds me that, though I've gone through many seasons in my heart, I made it through, and I'm going to keep moving until my time is done.

TALL, DARK, AND HANDSOME

Harcourt was the hub of everything happening, and I always had a front-row seat like a video recorder in the flesh. I paid attention when no one knew I was around because I stayed quiet—no one except Johnny Payne. I saw him in the neighborhood ever since we moved into the neighborhood but didn't pay him any attention.

Then, one day, when I was around sixteen, he came to our house looking for my younger brother and I answered the door. Little did I know he was really looking for me because one of the guys he hung around with wanted him to come and talk to me about him. Well, after speaking to me, he decided he was going to talk to me for himself and not his friend, but I didn't know it at the time.

Ozell would send me to the store where he worked part-time, and when I would go in, get what she wanted me to buy, and rush out, he would always seem to catch me before I did. Between his amazing smile and voice, they seemed to awaken parts in me I didn't know existed. After a while, I asked Ozell if she wanted me to go to the store just so he could notice me and seek me out.

He was tall, dark, and handsome as they say, and I was a skinny young thing with long hair and low self-esteem. I couldn't understand what he saw in me because I didn't dress fancy, nor did I wear makeup or jewelry at all. I always wanted to stay in the shadows but now someone was trying to pull me out into the light for all the world to see. After he pursued me for several months, I finally sat down with him and listened as he told me how beautiful I was and asked why I didn't smile a lot.

At this point, I didn't have much faith or trust in people, especially those of the male variety, because of what had happened. I always had my books to "escape" into and live through the lives of the characters in them. Even though my house was always full of people, I felt alone and abandoned. Until adulthood, I never told anyone about what happened with my stepfather, but eventually, I learned my sisters had similar experiences or worse.

After some time, we became friends, and one fateful day, I thought I was ready for something a little more, so I went to his parents' house while they were out of town. I don't know what I was thinking, but for some reason, I thought I was ready for intimacy. When he started to touch me, it didn't feel nasty, so I let him keep on, but when the time came to take my clothes off, I froze, jumped up, and ran all the way back to my house.

JUDY

My oldest sister Judy was home when I arrived, so I asked her if I could talk to her about something. She agreed and was nice enough to patiently listen to me. She asked if I was going all the way, and I said I couldn't. She said that meant I wasn't ready and not to let anyone try to convince me otherwise until I was. I loved Judy because she never judged me and always gave it to me straight. Thankfully, a bad choice was averted.

When I sit and think about it, I know I have made a lot of bad choices by this point in my life. Reflecting on how God was always there to help me make it through causes tears to well up in my eyes and a flutter in my heart. Even though my life had many challenges, which caused me a lot of pain, there were some great moments that brought me joy.

Chapter Three
BROKENNESS

TUCKED AWAY

It's strange to grow up in a house where all I wanted was to be loved. There were times when I may have felt it, but not from Ozell. I had a life that was full of joy and pain, and I guess that is what got me through because, without it, I don't think I would be as strong as I am today. Dealing with all the physical, sexual, and psychological abuse I did would have broken just about anyone and has broken many people. For a season or two, I was broken. I look back and see the times when just the sun shining down on me gave me a sense of joy and contentment that I thought I couldn't feel anymore. I reminded myself that God had not forgotten me.

For me, the simple things in life were smiles, laughter, feeling secure, loved, and wanted. I can visualize some of those fleeting moments in my heart's memory that manifested in different seasons of my life. Some I can retrace and some I have eulogized and buried in history's grave.

When I was young, I escaped life through books, and I was so proud when I got my first library card. I would get up on Saturday mornings and tell Ozell I was going to the library to get some books. The first book I ever checked out from the library was *Charlotte's Web*. I can't remember the other books I got, but I specifically remember getting *Charlotte's Web* with Wilbur the pig, Charlotte the spider, Templeton the rat, and let's not forget Fern.

There was a lot going on at that farm, but it reminded me of the wildness in my house with all the different characters and personalities that made up my family. When I came back home with my stack of books, I climbed up on the shelf in the clothes closet with my flashlight, burrowed under the clothes, and read my books until I fell asleep. After my sisters figured out where I was, the first time I disappeared in this spot, they would only check to make sure I was there but never disturbed me. I had so much fear from the abuse that books seemed to be my saving grace.

There was one time when all of us younger kids were having friends over since Ozell was gone for the weekend. We were all in the back bedroom hanging out when they began making fun of me because I was very thin and short for my age. They called me names, and it hurt so bad that I climbed into the wicker laundry basket and covered myself with the lid. Well, they thought that it would be fun to sit on top of the basket so that I couldn't get out. I didn't suffocate because of all the holes in it, but I cried for them to let me out while they all just laughed.

After a while, I grew tired, relaxed, and fell asleep inside. I guess after they didn't hear any noise for a while, they got scared and opened it only to find me sleeping. They thought I was unconscious, but I had accepted my fate and went straight to sleep. I guess I slept a lot when I was scared.

I did that a lot when things came against me, which was probably why people were able to take advantage of me. I didn't fight back. That is not the case today. Through God, my life has been strengthened, and I stand my ground because I am a force to be reckoned with. It is because of Jesus that I can stand tall and strong, and His grace has kept me from making wrong decisions that could've cost me my life or my freedom.

TEEN YEARS

One New Year's Eve, my Aunt Ida threw a party. I was close to her daughter, Robbie, at the time, and she was dating a guy named Michael, who had a cousin named Craig. On New Year's Eve, all the relatives were invited to her house to celebrate, so I decided to go with Judy, whom I did not spend a lot of time with growing up, but I loved her very much even though she was crazy sometimes.

We all had a wonderful time at the party, especially Judy. That was the first time I ever saw her dancing, which was crazy. While we were there, my cousin Robbie introduced me to Craig. However, he was distracted by a female friend on the phone. I didn't know at the time, but he was breaking up with her, so I left him to handle his business.

Midnight came, and everyone was going around hugging and wishing each other a Happy New Year. My cousin Robbie said I should go give Craig a hug, but I didn't know where he was. She told me where to find him, and I did. I waited for him to get off the phone since he was deep in conversation, and I just politely asked if I could give him a hug and wish him a Happy New Year. He paused for a second and said, "Yes."

I took the opportunity to plant a light kiss on his lips and said, "Happy New Year."

When I pulled back, he looked at me, smiled, and said, "Happy New Year to you, too."

He had the softest lips I had ever kissed. They felt like a soft cushiony, sweet-tasting piece of cotton candy. Lord, I'm blushing about how straightforward I was with him.

I then walked back into the living room and joined the party. I thought he must not have been interested in me, so, when it was time to leave, I said my goodbyes and got in the car with Judy. Little did I know that right after I left, Craig asked Robbie who I was and how he could get in touch with me. The next day, I slept in, and when I woke up, Donita said a guy named Craig called and asked if I could call him back. I took my time to return his call because I didn't want it to seem desperate. Y'all know what I mean.

I called him back the next day, and we started talking as friends. We asked each other general questions about our lives, and since I was a senior in high school, my answers were all about school and what I wanted to be and do after graduation. Craig didn't finish high school, so his responses were mostly about what he was doing each day.

One day, when I was leaving school, I came out, and low and behold, guess who was waiting for me out front. Craig said he wanted to walk me home, and I said, "Well, you had to take two buses to get here to do it."

We laughed and talked all the way to my house. This was the first of many trips Craig would make to my school and house. The first time Craig met Ozell was a week when she didn't go out gambling, and he came over. He had his mother call and ask my mother if they could pick me up from the house to go out to dinner with them, and she said yes, but she had to meet his parents first.

I don't know why because she was either at home sleeping or not at home at all for long periods of time. I guess she wanted them to believe she was concerned about her child. Craig came over with his stepfather and introduced themselves, and the only thing Ozell asked was if he had a brother for her. I was so embarrassed, but they laughed it off.

After we left, I thought we would go to a restaurant for dinner, but instead, we went to his family's home near the beach. It was a beautiful house in Pacific Palisades with a garage entrance that led into a secluded front yard. The front of the house had a beautiful wall of windows. His mom greeted me at the front door and was very polite throughout the time I was there. I guess she could tell I was very nervous and didn't say much because, in my mind, I didn't want to say the wrong thing.

After dinner, we sat and talked a bit. Craig's mother didn't ask too many personal questions, just about school and if I was going to college and what I was going to major in. I told her I wanted to be a lawyer, and she seemed pleased with my answer. She didn't ask me any questions about my family, and even if she did, I wouldn't have told her anything. She was a nice enough person to have respect and not pry into others' personal family lives. I liked her at first until after she married Craig's stepfather. They had a small, intimate ceremony with just their children and, a month later, invited others to a reception.

I got a job to take care of myself, and I only brought home $150.00 a week at the time, so I took $100.00 and bought his mother a crystal salt and pepper shaker, a crystal butter dish, and some other crystal items that I can't remember. I was so proud of the fact that I was even invited and then to be able to buy her what I thought were wonderful gifts, which I later found out she returned and got the money for. I tolerated her, for Craig's sake.

GRADUATION AND EARLY ADULTHOOD

Even though I was dating Craig, I still felt alone many times when I was not with him. I continued my trips to the library to check out books and went into the closet like I did when I was ten, but since I had grown a few inches, I couldn't climb onto the shelf with a flashlight anymore, so I hid under the hanging clothes and read until I fell asleep.

On June 23, 1978, it was graduation night at the Hollywood Palladium. We were going to the site but first made a pit stop. After the marines, Gary got into some trouble and had to go to prison. He did three-and-a-half years and when released, he had to go to a halfway house before he could come home, and I wanted him to see me before I graduated.

When we arrived, he came to the front of the building to congratulate Donita and me since we were graduating together. After hugging him and hearing him tell us he was proud of us, we got in Ozell's Lincoln Mark V and drove to the ceremony. They called our names right after each other, and we went down at the same time and received our diplomas together.

As a surprise, Craig showed up and sat with my family. Afterward, we all went back to the house and celebrated, and then the hammer came down. Ozell told both of us that after graduation day, we were responsible for our own wellbeing. I was seventeen at the time, and she was still receiving welfare for me until November. Despite that small detail, I decided to get a job and start taking care of myself.

My first job was at Prudential Life Insurance in the mail room. I also started taking classes at Santa Monica City College. I worked during the day, and at night, I spent time with Craig. By this time, we were intimate, so it seemed we were well on our way to having a full relationship. I remember the first time I spent the night at his family's home that he grew up in.

His mother, who remarried years after Craig's father passed away, gave the family home to Craig, his older brother Frank, and his older sister as she moved into the Pacific Palisades house with her new husband. Craig's sister, who was an aspiring model, and brother were nice to me, but because of what I had gone through, I wasn't too trusting.

I decided to leave Prudential, start going to city college more, and move out into my own apartment. Craig decided to enlist in the Navy so we could start our future together. Little did I know that the future I envisioned was not what was in store for me. I found a place in the jungle (what we called Baldwin Hills). It was okay for just me and Craig when he came home from the military.

After he went to basic training, he had his graduation in San Diego, California, and his family was going down there to see him. He thought I was going to stay at home, but I surprised him and went with them. I watched him as he marched in formation. He looked so handsome, but they cut off all those long curls he had. His family was Creole, but he looked more white than black. He had these long curls I would twirl my fingers through until I reached the end. Even with them gone, he was still the most handsome man on that field.

WHY ME?

We had a good start with him being in the Navy and me working for us to move forward until the ship he was assigned to was scheduled to go out to Westpac, which meant they were going to go out to sea for eleven months. I wanted to spend as much time with him as possible until he had to leave, but three days before he was to leave, he disappeared, and I didn't get to see him until the night before he left.

I was so hurt by this unexplained absence that he spent the last night with me. Ultimately, he missed his ship when it left port, and I knew that was the end of our relationship. Not knowing where he was or who he was with for three days made me realize I was not his primary concern. Because of that betrayal, it was easy to pull away since I wouldn't see him for almost a year.

I didn't trust or fall in love easily, but when I did, I opened my heart and took a chance with Craig. Later, I learned from his sister-in-law that he was with another woman those three days, but once he left, I didn't care anymore. Knowing this caused me to tear my heart from him. When he first left, I wrote to him two to three times a day, but after finding out he cheated, the letters slowed down until I finally stopped writing altogether.

I was only eighteen and had experienced so much hurt that by the time I broke up with him, I readily gave up on men and decided to make myself a priority for the first time in my life. I re-enrolled in community college and took a couple of courses to help me decide what career path I wanted to pursue.

After he was gone, I started enjoying my newfound singlehood. I took care of myself! started to feel myself come alive for the first time in a long time. I dated a few times just to have some company, but I was not interested in anything serious. The guys at the club were just for entertainment and free drinks. I had no man and no children. My only responsibility was me.

I remember dating one of the cute guys in the neighborhood named Michael, who I had known since I moved there. Little did I know that he was not the faithful kind either. I called my cousin to see if she wanted to hang out and found out Michael was there with her. They met because, one day, my cousin needed a ride home, so I asked him if we could take her. I was unaware they exchanged information and began seeing each other.

When I found out from my aunt that he was there, I told her I was dating him and didn't understand how they could do that to me. My aunt was so furious that she made him leave, and I didn't deal with either of them other anymore. That wasn't the last time that she did this to me, but I didn't find out until years later.

Once again, I decided to be alone for a season, and it felt good to just enjoy myself. I went where I wanted and hung out with whomever I wanted. I requested no accountability and gave none in return. Donita was the only person I shared and trusted with everything. We spent a lot of time just talking about where we wanted to take our lives and how we survived what we went through at home. But life in that house wasn't done with me yet.

Chapter Four

LONGING

FROM ONE TRAUMA TO ANOTHER

One day, I was in Ozell's house with my other siblings, just chit-chatting, and Ozell walked into the room visibly upset for some unknown reason. This time, I was the one she zeroed in on. I instantly knew I was her target but didn't know why. I stood there next to Gary with fear and trembling, but not in a biblical sense. She started cursing at everyone and then turned and started cursing me out. I didn't say a word, which I guess made her even angrier because she came over to me.

I started backing up until I backed myself into the corner, where she proceeded to punch me in the face and chest. At first, I let her hit me, but because the pain from the punches was so great, I didn't know what to do. I just put my hands up to block her from punching my lights out. Gary pulled her away from me, and I stood there crying, asking what I had done, but she never gave me an answer.

She yelled that I was trying to fight her back, but I wasn't. I was trying to keep her from breaking my nose or giving me a black eye like she did to Donita back in the day. When we were younger, Ozell went to whip Donita and grabbed the belt, but it was the loose end and she swung and hit Donita in the eye with the buckle. Her eye immediately swelled shut, but Ozell never took her to the doctor for fear of them finding out she was abusive. From that day on, Donita was legally blind in her left eye.

After that incident, Ozell gave me thirty minutes to pack my things and leave her house. I told her I had nowhere to go, and she said she didn't care and to get out of her house. Since I was friends with my cousin's girlfriend, I asked them if I could stay with them, and thankfully they said yes. Little did I know trauma was just starting to heat up.

I packed my bags and moved in with them, but it turned out to be an apartment full of horrors. Each night, I was awakened by my cousin's girlfriend screaming for him to stop beating her. The first night, I jumped up and went to the door and asked if everything was okay. She said yes, but I could hear him telling her to be quiet, or he would punch her again.

I yelled for him to stop, but when he opened the door, I could see her upper chest had multiple bruises on it. She was very fair-skinned and bruised very easily. She also had a large lump just above her breasts and that's where he would hit her knowing it was more painful when he hit her there.

DEVASTATION

I thought this was worse than staying at Ozell's house, but things took yet another darker turn for me. One night, while I was sleeping on the sofa, I was awakened by a hand moving between my legs. I was so scared that it paralyzed me. I pretended to sleep hard and didn't move, so after my cousin finished touching me with his hands, he climbed on my back and started raping me. I couldn't move, so I just snored loudly and acted like I never woke up.

This continued for four or five nights until I couldn't take it anymore. I told Gary, and he said he was going to come over to see for himself what was going on. Well, he came over and realized I was not going to be safe there and spoke to Ozell, who said I needed to come back home. When I returned home, she never asked me if I was okay or what happened. It broke my heart but at least I wasn't in the monster's house anymore. From then on, I made sure to stay out of Ozell's sight, fearing she might attack me or put me out again.

As time went on, I started a new job, spent time with myself, and finally started to make myself happy when an old flame returned from overseas. One day, I felt like going to the park. The sun was out, and there was a cool breeze, so I thought it was a good time to relax at the neighborhood park called Vineyard Park. I left Ozell's house and started down the street, and before

I could make it past the first block, I heard someone call my name. I turned around to see who it was, and to my surprise, it was Johnny Payne. When I think about it now, I should've said hello and kept walking because little did I know that detour would forever change my life and not in the best way possible.

My mind told me to keep walking, but he looked so fine that I had to go back and see what he wanted. I told him I didn't know that he was back in town and asked where his wife, whom he married in high school, was. I didn't go after him because I understood marriage and was not going to be the one to cross that line or allow him to cross it with me.

He said that they were getting a divorce because while he was away for a year, he found out she was cheating on him with another man and spending all the money he was sending her with the other guy while he was gone. My first thought was *Yay*, but then I came to my senses and said I was sorry he was going through this. I said goodbye and went on my way to the park. While I walked away, I nervously wondered if he was watching me go. When I turned around, I thought to myself, *Oh yes, he's watching me.* This time was different, I wasn't fearful and felt like I was given another chance with the first person I fell in love with.

NEW ADVENTURES

After spending the afternoon at the park, I decided to walk home, which happened to pass Johnny's parents' home. I guess he stayed outside to see if I would come by again, and when I did, he stopped me. We sat there for hours, reminiscing about what had been going on in our lives. He asked me if I was dating anyone, and I said yes, but he was on Westpac with the Navy. That was a lie, but I didn't want him to think I was available now.

Johnny was also in the Navy, and he had just gotten back from Westpac a couple of weeks prior. He wanted to surprise his wife, but he ended up being the one surprised. I also told him I had been cheated on just before my boyfriend left and was not interested in getting into another relationship, on top of the fact that Johnny was still married.

I went home, and the next day he came around the corner to my house. We sat outside under the carport and talked some more. I explained that he hurt me when we were younger because he knew I had strong feelings for him but failed to tell me he had gotten married. I said we could be friends and he seemed okay for the moment.

We kept spending time together, and over time, he wore my defenses down until I did what I said I would not do. I gave in sexually, and all those locked-away feelings came rushing back but in a different, more adult way. I explained I couldn't do that anymore as long as he was married but after a few times, the damage was done. My heart totally belonged to him.

Months went by and Craig's return was approaching. I called his sister's house to see if he had returned so I could tell him we were over, but instead found out he had been back for three weeks already. That was the answer I needed, so I moved on with my life and Johnny.

We started dating and after a few months, I asked him about his divorce. He said it was in process, even though I never saw any documentation. He was still in the Navy and stationed near San Francisco, California, on the USS Kansas City. He came down on weekends so we could spend time together. I really had a thing for a man in uniform.

One day, while Johnny was back on his ship, Craig decided to show up at Ozell's house and we spent some time talking about how things turned out. He asked for another chance and even asked me to marry him, but by this time, I was over him and ready to start a new life with Johnny. What Craig didn't know was that Johnny already asked me to move to Oakland, California, to be closer to him, and I said yes because there was nothing holding me back in Los Angeles. I talked to Donita about it, and she said I should go for it.

On the day I packed and got ready to head to the airport, guess who showed up...Craig. He called previously, and Donita told him I was leaving, and if he was serious about getting me back, he had to make it quick. He came with an engagement ring and asked me to marry him while I was still packing my clothes to leave. He even rode all the way to the airport with me and my other brother Ricky to try to stop me from leaving, but I was determined to get away.

He watched as I checked in and then walked me all the way to the gate until I boarded the plane. I told him to give the engagement ring to someone else, and I left him standing there with it in his hand. I guess he realized the mistake he had made, but it was too little, too late.

As I sat on the plane, I realized it was the first time I had ever been on an airplane, and I was nervous yet excited to start a new adventure. Finally, my plane landed, and when I deboarded, my legs felt like jelly because I didn't relax the whole time. Johnny's cousin met me at the airport and allowed me to stay at her house until I was able to get situated. Johnny showed up after he got off duty, and he said he couldn't believe I would come simply because he asked me to. He said he had always tried to get his ex-wife to relocate, but she was too scared to leave her neighborhood. I was always adventurous, so to me, this was another opportunity to see a new part of California.

I stayed at her house for about a month while I looked for a job and an apartment for Johnny and me to stay in. It didn't take long for the honeymoon stage to end of staying in someone else's home. There were definite facial expressions, under-the-breath statements, and then a full-blown argument came. Luckily, I had already landed a job, and since we already had money saved up before I went to Oakland, it was easy for us to move. I wanted a fresh start and to be able to carve out a little slice of happiness. I thought moving there would bring me what I was looking for, but little did I know that was all in my head, not his.

NAIVE

I never took him for a cheater, but I was so naive thinking I found my knight in shining armor. I guess I had read too many books and thought I could live like that in real life. The first time he was unfaithful was with a female who I thought was a friend, but it turns out they both were like rabid dogs. One day, I came home early from work because I wasn't feeling good, and when I arrived, my friend Virginia was in our apartment, wearing a shirt with no bra, shorts, and no panties. You see, Virginia lived in the same apartment complex as us, and we also worked at the same office. I was a receptionist, and she was a counselor for individuals recently released from incarceration.

She had called out from work, but I didn't think anything of it, and Johnny didn't have duty that day, so he stayed home as well. Naive again. When I walked in and found her in our apartment, I asked her what she was doing there. She said she was waiting for me to come home, but she was acting funny. I was too nervous to ask the real question. I looked at him, and she said it was no big deal, so I forced myself to let it go. I told her it was time for her to go home because I didn't feel good, and she left.

When we were by ourselves, I questioned him, and he said my sickness had me imagining things. We argued, and I told him this was not what I came to Oakland for, and if this was the lifestyle he wanted, he could do it by himself. He kept saying he didn't cheat, and he understood how the situation could have looked that way. He also knew I wasn't the type to have people at my house (especially females) when I wasn't home. The next day at work, I had a conversation with Virginia and told her she was no longer welcome at my house whether I was there or not. That friendship ended quickly, and I felt better when she quit.

I woke up one morning and wasn't feeling like myself, so I called out from work. I went to the doctor to see if I had the flu, and to my surprise, I found out I was pregnant. I left the doctor's office having mixed emotions because I felt I was too young to be a mother, and at the same time, I felt that my unborn child should not have to pay the price for my decision not to use protection. I took the bus home since we didn't have a car, and while I was riding, all I could think of was what I was going to do, all the while never considering Johnny's position.

After I made it to our apartment, I opened a jar of pickles and ate the whole thing. I began to understand what morning sickness was. I spent the rest of the day sick in the bathroom. It was 5:30 p.m., and Johnny finally made it home and was asking if dinner was ready, but after he saw the sorry state I was in, he asked if I was okay. I was so nervous that I didn't know how to tell him what the doctor said. Having had so much sorrow in my life, I always saw things as half-empty.

After looking at him for a couple of minutes I started crying. Nervously, he picked me up, carried me to the bedroom, and told me to rest. He went to the store down the hill and bought me some soda, crackers, and soup. After he came back, he asked what was wrong, and with a nervous voice I said, "I'm pregnant."

He looked at me and started smiling. Suddenly, my frown turned into a smile, and we started talking about getting a larger apartment since we were in a one-bedroom. I told him to slow down because I was only two months along, and we had time to figure things out. I spent a couple of days getting myself together, and when I went back to work, the company was downsizing and not only did I find out I was pregnant, but I was also out of a job.

To top it all off, Johnny's wife, whom he had not yet divorced, contacted him and asked if she could come up to where he was for a month to see if they could work it out once she found out I was there. First of all, I couldn't believe he was telling me this right after we found out we were pregnant, but he had the nerve to utter the next sentence to me.

He asked me to move out of my own apartment and let her move in. I said I was going to move out and back down to Los Angeles, and he could do whatever he wanted. The glass that was half empty was now staring me in the face, so I decided to drink the rest of it and move back to Ozell's house in Los Angeles and begin my next season as a single mother.

His wife never moved up there, and I decided, even though I didn't want to, I would be a single parent. A couple of weeks went by, and Johnny came to Ozell's house to see if I was okay. I told him I didn't need him anymore and wished him and his wife a wonderful life. He said that if I didn't talk to him, he was going to take my baby when it was born, and he and his wife would raise it. I cussed him out, ran inside Ozell's house, and slammed the door. Gary came out and told him that if he ever spoke to me like that again, he was going to come up missing, and since my family were gang members, he meant it.

When I was five months pregnant, I sat in Ozell's front yard since she allowed me to return home. Johnny's father, Mr. Payne, walked by and noticed I was pregnant. He asked me about it, and I told him the truth about who the father was. He was surprised and asked why I didn't tell him. I said, "Since Johnny was getting back with his wife, I didn't want to be a part of that whole situation."

He seemed sad and walked home, but later that day, Mrs. Payne called and asked if I could come by their apartment to talk. I said I would. Once I got there, they never asked me if Johnny was the father, they just asked if they could be a part of the baby's life, and I said yes. They were always nice to me, and since they wanted grandchildren, they were elated to know one was on the way.

One day while I was visiting them, Johnny's wife came over and found me there and was trying to get Mr. and Mrs. Payne to come to her side because she was still Johnny's wife even though they were separated. Mr. Payne told her that since I was carrying his grandchild, I was their priority and not her. She started crying and said I was ruining her life and left, but they didn't care. All they wanted was a grandchild since they were now in their fifties.

For the first time in my life, I felt loved, even though it was only because I was pregnant. I took full advantage of my position and enjoyed the rest of my pregnancy. Once Johnny found out his parents knew I was pregnant, he decided to end his season of stupidity and wanted to be a part of his child's life especially knowing it was a boy.

NEW LIFE

Once a month, Johnny flew or took the bus down from his station in San Francisco to Los Angeles to bring me things for the baby and money to ensure I had everything I needed. He also apologized for what happened in Oakland regarding his wife whom he had divorced by the time our son was born. Even though I was optimistic, I still had my guard up regarding trusting him fully.

Ozell didn't allow Johnny to stay in the house when he came for his visits. Thankfully, Gary had a van he kept in the backyard that we called the Blue Goose. I ran an extension cord from the house to the van so we could have heat and light while we lived there. I loved the Blue Goose because I could relax and not worry about what was going on inside of the house and stay out of Ozell's sight. I spent countless hours reminiscing and talking to my growing baby bump until August 18, 1980, when my beautiful, precious baby boy decided to enter the world.

I stayed at Ozell's house for about a year after Johnny Jr. was born so we could bond and give him a full-time mom, but as fate would have it, I had to get a job a little sooner than that. When he was nine months old, I was hired by an insurance company and decided it was time the baby and I moved into our own place. By this time, my son's father was discharged from the Navy due to Mr. Payne having had a heart attack. Johnny didn't want to be so far away from us or his parents. He was given a hardship discharge.

Life was wonderful until I found out I was pregnant with our second child, and Johnny Sr. started having a wandering eye again. I found out it was a girl, and at first, I considered terminating the pregnancy since I had already terminated two prior to conceiving her. But Johnny begged me not to and said this was the girl he wanted so badly.

When little Johnny was twelve months old, Ozell had suspicions about him because of her experience with my sister Linda. We scheduled a doctor's appointment and found out he was, in fact, special needs. Even though I didn't care (because he was God's gift to me), Johnny Sr. started to spend less time with him than before his diagnosis.

The insurance company I worked for did drug screenings. After giving me one, they came and informed me of my second pregnancy but didn't terminate my employment. Back then, they could since there was no law protecting pregnant women from being terminated. I started in the mailroom, opening and sorting mail for different departments until it was time for me to deliver my second blessing from God.

I was originally going to name her Rozell Renee, after my mother and sister Rose (who couldn't have children), but before I could sign her name on the birth certificate, Johnny came up to the hospital and told me he heard this name and wanted to see if I would change it to Tanisha instead. Well, after looking at her for a couple of minutes I said, "Do you want to be called Tanisha instead?"

I swear she smiled when I said that, so from then on her name was Tanisha Renee. I didn't find out until we broke up that the mysterious name came from a woman he cheated on me with while I was pregnant. From that day forward, my family and I called her Cookie instead.

SEVERING TIES

I also found out during this period that he was cheating on me with my childhood best friend, a female at my job, and a couple more at his job. When I confronted him about it, he became physically abusive. The day after I came home from the hospital from having Tanisha, Donita visited our apartment. Johnny and I started arguing, so she got up and went home leaving me to deal with the fallout. I wonder to this day why she left me in that situation, or better yet, why I left myself in it.

One thing led to another, and he slapped me so hard that I fell to the floor. When I tried to get up, he was sitting on my stomach. Yes, the same stomach that had just given birth to his child the day before. All six feet, two inches, and 210 pounds pressed down on my 125 pounds until I passed out. When I came to, he was still sitting on me and cussing me out. Sadly, he didn't even know I had passed out until I woke up and wondered what happened.

It wasn't until that moment that my heart started changing toward him, and even though I still loved him, I didn't like him anymore. The only reason that I continued to stay was because I didn't want to be like my mother, with multiple kids and no father around. Crazy, huh? I continued to make the best of it until one day, I was at home and the phone rang. A woman asked to speak to Johnny, so I asked her name. She said it was Pat. I asked her what she wanted with Johnny, and she said she wanted to come see him. I asked her if she knew he had a family and that I had just given birth a couple of months ago. She said he told her I would be over at his apartment sometimes with the babies. I responded that it was my apartment, and if she could come over, I would confront him right in front of her.

Lo and behold, this crazy girl came over one night and sat on my sofa right in front of me. I said to myself, *Is she crazy or something? Didn't she know that I could do anything to her?* She waited until Johnny came home, and he walked right into this one. The look on his face was priceless. She played it cool though, while he acted like I was visiting his place when really it was my apartment that he moved into with me.

He was even bold enough to tell me to my face that he didn't want to be with me anymore and even though his words cut like a knife to my heart, I didn't want to give him or her the satisfaction of knowing it. I said "Okay, now you can move out of my apartment and back in with your parents."

After a while, she left, and Johnny and I started arguing. This time, I decided it was time and told him I was leaving him, and he could start his new life with Pat. He didn't take that news so well. He went into the kids' bedroom, and since our son was a deep sleeper even as a toddler, Johnny grabbed him by his long, curly hair, put a knife up to his throat, and said that if I left him he would cut little Johnny's throat.

I tried to reason with him and said I just needed to take a walk and was going to take the babies with me, but he insisted I leave them asleep and go cool off. Even though I was scared to leave them, I prayed he would not truly hurt them. So, I walked around the corner to Ozell's house since we lived only a couple of blocks away.

I went inside and told her what had just happened. She said she was not going to help until I took the first step—call the police. I did, and when they reached her house, lo and behold, she knew them personally. She politely asked them to teach him a lesson about abuse, and they nodded their heads.

We got into the car and followed the police but quickly noticed his car was parked at his parents' apartment driveway. I got out and told the officers about his car, and they told me to stay where I was. When they reached the car, my babies were left inside it while he was inside the apartment. This fool left my babies inside a locked car by themselves, and they were only twenty-one months and two months old.

When he heard the noise coming from downstairs, he came out, and the police asked him his name and if those were his children. He said yes. They then asked me to get out of the car and identify him, and I did. He started walking toward the car with my babies inside when the police told him to stay away from the car or they would taze him. He started cussing them out, so they grabbed him, threw him on the car, handcuffed him, and placed him under arrest for child endangerment. I then realized I was severing my ties with him. Even though we had children together, my heart was starting to feel the tear and it hurt so much that I thought I was going to have a heart attack.

I decided to stay at Ozell's house that night with the babies because I didn't want to go back there in case he got out. He kept calling Ozell's house, begging me to drop the charges, and I told him no. Plus, Ozell said that if I went back to him, she wouldn't help me anymore. I stuck to my guns.

The next morning, I got ready to go to work, leaving my babies at Ozell's with Donita since she still lived there. After I made it to work, I received a phone call. It was Ozell who was frantic on the other end saying, CPS (Child Protective Services) came due to the arrest and took my children and didn't tell her where they were. I immediately went home and called the number on the card. All they could tell me was the children were taken because of the seriousness of the situation. I had to go to court seven days later. Do you know what that did to my heart and mind? I didn't know if they were okay? If they were together? If they were being hurt? Lord!

Chapter Five
FAMILY

LONGEST SEVEN DAYS

My babies, my life, were gone, and I didn't know what to do. I felt like giving up and letting go of life. "Donita, what do I do?" I said, crying on her shoulder.

She kept telling me not to give up. She understood what I was going through because when they came to take my babies, she was holding my little two-month-old Tanisha in her arms. I frantically called every number at the state and didn't get anywhere. I only heard that I had to go to court in seven days. Seven days was like a lifetime away. How was I supposed to sleep or eat? I kept biting my nails until they bled while fear saturated every inch of my body. All of this was because of Johnny, who didn't even come by to see if I was okay after he found out my babies were gone. He came to court to find out what was going to happen to him and not my babies.

Finally, the court day came around, and I couldn't wait to hold my babies again. Ozell went with me to ensure that I got my children back no matter what. I had never been to court a day in my life, and there I was, sitting before a judge who had the power to tell me that either I could or couldn't hold my babies again.

Johnny sat over there smugly but wouldn't dare look at Ozell at all because he knew she meant what she said. The judge addressed us both and said my children could come home only if I stayed at my mother's house because she had supervision over them for a month while we BOTH went to anger management. My children and I were the victims, but I still had to take a class for them to be released to me. I agreed, and as Ozell signed the documents, I looked over at him with extreme hatred in my eyes. He smiled like he had won.

When my mother and I left the courtroom and walked down the hall, she passed him and said, "If I see you again, I'm going to kill you."

The look on his face said it all. I just started laughing and walked out with Ozell to get my babies. He wanted to know where the babies were, but we just kept walking until we reached her car. After we got in, she said that the children were split up and sent to separate foster homes. She said that since Tanisha was the closest to get to then we were going to go and get her first. I don't know why, but my greatest concern was for my son since he was a toddler with special needs and didn't know anyone else except me.

We finally reached Tanisha, who was being looked after by a black family, but they didn't know why she was even there as they noted she looked well cared for. We told them what happened, and they suggested I should try to live a separate life from him since he almost cost me everything meaningful. I agreed, and when I held my baby girl, all the stress that had built up in my body started to diminish, but not completely, because I was still very concerned about little Johnny. He was almost two hours away. When we pulled up to the house, it looked like it was not very well kept, and when we got out of the car to go inside, Ozell said to stay in the living room and not ask any questions.

When we left the house to go to court, my mother had me pack clean clothes, a washcloth, a change of diapers, and a trash bag for them. I didn't know why, but when we got to where Johnny was, I started to understand. I think my mother had been through this scenario before with one or more of my older siblings so she knew what we might encounter and didn't want me to go off and lose my chance of taking my babies home.

Ozell went into the other room with the older white lady while I waited with bated breath as she brought my son to me. He was only wearing a diaper that had turned orange from the urine that had built up inside it from them not changing him. After I grabbed him, Ozell held Tanisha and told us to get up and leave without saying anything to the lady. Before we walked out, I did turn and give her a look that could've killed her but said nothing to her.

After we got into the car, I put Tanisha in her car seat, and then I turned to Johnny, I laid the trash bag down on the back seat, took off the dirty diaper, and began to wash him with the bottle of water, baby bath, and then I lotioned him up, put clean clothes on him, and started to hug and kiss him everywhere. He didn't cry but only held onto me tightly. When I looked into those brown almond-shaped eyes, all I could see was unconditional love looking back at me. I promised him I would never be separated from him and his sister again. When I sat him down on the chair, I picked up Tanisha and held her close to him, and all he kept saying was, "Baa baa." He kissed and hugged her, and from that day, I did everything in my power to ensure we were never separated from each other again.

MOVING AGAIN AND AGAIN

After we made it back to Ozell's house, I asked if I could stay while I looked for another place for me and the kids, and she said yes. I found another apartment, and Johnny had to move back into his parents' house because, after that situation, the owners of the property, who knew Ozell, evicted him. I moved down the street from my old apartment because it was a close distance to Ozell's and Mr. and Mrs. Payne's homes, and I could drop the babies off at the Payne's after Johnny went to work and pick them back up before he got home.

Well, as time would have it, I eventually let my guard down again. I know what you're thinking. I guess I was still holding out hope that things would get better if I gave him one more chance. To no one's surprise, after I let him move in with us, he started cheating. This time I decided to move on for good because I found out that he was cheating with Pat again. I moved out of my apartment and far enough away that he wouldn't come there. I finally had my babies, and we were happy for once. Don't get me wrong, financially, it was a struggle, but we were making it.

I ended up moving into a one-bedroom apartment in Baldwin Hills that was just big enough for the kids and me. I liked my new place even though I didn't have any furniture. Johnny wouldn't even let me take my daughter's crib instead he gave it to someone else. I stopped caring about it and him and focused on my children and them spending time with their grandparents.

Mr. and Mrs. Payne were wonderful. I had to take two buses to work each day and one of the stops was not far from their house, so Mr. Payne would meet me there with a shopping cart for the babies and walk them back to his home. He had several blankets for them to lay on and made it seem as if they were going on an adventure each day.

When they saw Mr. Payne, their faces lit up like they had just seen heaven; his would do the same when he saw them. Of course, Johnny had a car, yet wouldn't even drive his dad to the bus stop to pick them up. What a scumbag. You know, when you think you're in love, you don't see the dark side. You only see what you want to see. But when the scales are removed from your eyes, the world seems a lot different—sometimes better and sometimes worse.

MY HEART HURTS

One day, my kids' grandparents wanted me to bring the kids over so they could spend some time with them because they were planning on moving back to their home state of Louisiana soon. I didn't have a car, but I had a closed-in stroller that kept the sun and rain off them. I packed them up and walked over to their place. When I got there, Johnny was there and wanted to talk, but I was not in the mood to deal with him. I took the kids upstairs to Mr. and Mrs. Payne, and when I came back downstairs to leave, he grabbed my arm and I pulled away from him. He said he wanted to see if we could try again, and I said emphatically, no!

I guess that was not the answer he wanted, so he slapped me, and for the first time, I fought back with all my strength no matter how futile it was. After I punched him back, he slapped me so hard that I fell to the ground. He then started kicking me in my side with his boots, and once I knew I couldn't get back up, I curled into a fetal position to protect myself until he stopped. His parents yelled at him to stop, or they would call the police.

I got up and ran fast to Ozell's house, and I was okay to leave my babies because his parents had already kicked him out on the street. They wouldn't let him in to see the kids. His father even pointed a rifle at him and told him to leave. After I made it to Ozell's house, my brothers were there, and when they went around the corner, Johnny was gone. The streets were looking for him, though. After a couple of days, I gathered up my babies, said goodbye to Mr. and Mrs. Payne, and assured them I would not keep the kids from them.

One day after work, I went to see Donita, who stayed at my brother Albert's house. I needed to talk to her because I was being evicted from my apartment for non-payment. I had a nervous breakdown and began cutting myself, so I went on short-term disability, which cut my income down by a third. I admitted myself to a mental hospital for a week because of the stress, abuse, and assaults. It felt like my life bottlenecked, and I cried out to the Lord. I was ready to end it all for good.

You see, Johnny kept me in court filing for child support because he was refusing to pay. I spent my entire two-week vacation that year going back and forth to court for him to pay only two hundred dollars a month for two children. While I was talking to Donita, Albert said I could stay with them since he had enough room for all of us, and he wasn't there most of the time. I agreed and moved in for a short while before getting something close by for me and my kids soon after.

Little did I know that my brother Albert was working on paying Johnny back for what he did to me and the children. Since Albert allegedly sold drugs, he allegedly gave Johnny some crack for free to get him hooked since he already smoked pot. Well, it only took Johnny one hit to get hooked, and he began allegedly buying it from him.

I was over at Albert's place with the kids one day, and Johnny came over to buy drugs. Since he hadn't seen his kids in a couple of years, he didn't recognize them right away. Albert set him up to humiliate him in the best (or worst, depending upon your point of view) possible way. We were sitting on the sofa in the living room facing the front door, and when Albert opened the door, Johnny couldn't see in because of the bar doors on the outside of the solid door.

Once Albert knew my eyes were fixed on the door, he opened it up, and Johnny stepped inside. My eyes met his, and I was instantly shocked at what I saw. He was wearing a white FILA® sweatsuit and trying to allegedly buy drugs from my brother. My son recognized him, hopped off my lap, and ran to meet him. It took Johnny a couple of seconds to realize who was grabbing his leg. He patted little Johnny on the head and then proceeded to allegedly negotiate for some drugs.

Johnny didn't have any money, so Albert asked about the FILA sweatsuit he was wearing. Johnny said he would be right back. He left and came back an hour later wearing some old, ragged overalls and a dirty t-shirt and handed Albert the sweat suit for the exchange. He left without acknowledging his children at all. I realized then I had dodged a major bullet.

I went back across the street to my new apartment and began working on getting myself some furniture. I was at home sitting on the floor one day, and the doorbell rang. I got up to see who it was, and Albert told me to open the door. I did so I could see what Johnny wanted. He had all my furniture I had to leave behind after Johnny and I split up a couple of years prior and brought it into my place. Johnny was so far gone in his addiction that he traded everything he had, including my stuff. God was still looking out for me.

ACCEPTING DEFEAT

My babies and I were living in what we called the Jungle in Los Angeles, in a one-bedroom apartment on the second floor. One night, at the club with Donita and our friends, I met a guy ten years my senior. He seemed nice or maybe I was just desperate for someone to notice me that I took it as him being attracted to me. Dale, a 33-year-old, who reminded me of the leader of the Gap Band, came and introduced himself, and we spent some time talking. I gave him my phone number, and he called me a few days later.

We talked, and I invited him over for dinner. For some stupid reason, I had my babies there when he came. I introduced him to them and sent them to bed after they had dinner and baths. Dale and I sat up half the night talking and eventually fell asleep. Nothing sexual happened. He slept in the living room, and I slept in the bedroom with my babies, with the door closed and locked. When I got up the next morning, he was already gone, but he left a note that he enjoyed the time.

A little while later, my children stayed with their grandparents because I had a cold and didn't want to pass it on to them.

Dale came over, and when he found out I was sick, he made me some soup and spent the night again. I fell asleep in his arms. He again left before I woke up with another note. After a little more time, we became sexually involved. By this time, my babies were eighteen months and two and a half years old and were spending the weekend at their grandparents' house. This made it easy for me to let him stay over.

Things soon took a turn I didn't see coming. I let him stay at my apartment while I went to work overtime. When I came home, he said that since I was letting him stay there while I wasn't there, he had a spare key made for himself. This was without my permission, which caught me so off guard. I was nervous and too afraid to say anything. He wasn't violent, but this made my antenna go up.

I should have said he didn't have my permission, but instead, I simply said, "Okay." What an idiot I was to not stop him before it was too late. Luckily, my older sister Judy needed a place to stay, and I welcomed her even though she was a drug addict. She never hurt me or my children, and I knew she loved me regardless of her personal struggles. Dale and I dated for about six months before all hell broke loose.

One night, Johnny came to see the kids, and I got tired, so I told him I was going to bed since he was still talking to Judy in the living room. When I woke up the next morning to get the kids ready, Johnny was still there asleep in the living room. I woke him up and asked why he stayed there. He said that while he and Judy were talking, they fell asleep.

He agreed to take the kids to his parents' house so I could get ready for work. I knew he would not hurt the babies. I called Mr. Payne and told him Johnny was bringing them his way. When I was leaving work, Mr. Payne asked if the kids could stay the night, and since I always packed more than enough clothing for them, I said yes. By the time I made it home, Judy was gone, and Dale was standing in the living room with the spare key in his hand. He asked if the kids' father spent the night, and I explained what happened. I guess Judy told him another story and left. He called me all sorts of names and said I was only worth a thousand dollars, threw the key down on the floor, and walked out.

I didn't know what had happened, and without knowing where Judy was to ask her what had taken place, I started to go dark within myself. I thought he cared about me, but the reality is that I wasn't paying attention to the signs of who he really was. I later found out that he was hooked on an ADHD drug called Ritalin but didn't have the disorder. I allowed the devil to speak to my heart and tell me to sacrifice my life. Since I was such a depressed and damaged person, I should save my children from having to live with a person like me.

I listened to that mess and tried to cut my left forearm with a butter knife. When that didn't do anything, I found a razor blade instead. I must have hit two veins because there were two spouts of blood shooting up like a fountain that slowly flowed down my arm like a stream. All I could think of at the time was, *Wow, blood really is warm.*

After all the pain I suffered in my life, I felt I had reached my end. While the blood was running down my arm, I followed the same voice that told me to go into the kitchen and grab a steak knife. The voice said to put it up to my heart and end my suffering; all I had to do was thrust it into my chest and it would all be over.

I held the knife up to my chest and tried to do a soft jab, but it only went skin deep before I stopped due to it hurting. I threw the knife down and screamed out, "Jesus! Help me!" I immediately lost consciousness and was awakened by someone in my apartment, even though I knew no one was there. This female person was very gentle with me, and as I lay on the floor, she put my head on her lap and stroked my forehead. She then put a bandage on my forearm and after she kissed me on the forehead, I fell back asleep.

When I woke up the next morning, my arm was bandaged, but I had no memory of who had done it. I began experiencing missing gaps of time. I remember getting up but not getting dressed, being at the bus stop but not knowing how I got there, getting off the bus at work but not the ride, and getting off the elevator at work but not the elevator itself.

My next real memory was of me sitting at my desk and my boss checking to see if I was okay because, apparently, people were talking to me, but I didn't respond. When she touched me, I jumped and looked up at her. She asked me if my arm was okay because there was blood soaking through it, and when I looked at it, I told her I didn't know what happened.

She asked, "Can I look at it?"

I said, "Yes."

When she rolled up my sleeve, she had this shocked look on her face and asked, "Who did this?"

I couldn't answer her. She took me to her office, took off the old bandage, cleaned my forearm, and rewrapped it. She told me that I had to go to the hospital to get it checked out, and like a little child, I said OK.

I don't remember leaving my job, but I do recall the cold air outside. I saw a couple of buildings on the way to the hospital as I rode the bus. I only remember walking into the hospital and saying, "My boss said I should come here."

I was taken into a room where a nurse said he would have to stick a needle in my arm to numb it. I said, "Okay," but didn't feel anything.

As I lay there wondering why I was there, the nurse kept asking me questions I didn't have answers for. He said, "Wait here until the doctor comes in."

CRYING OUT FOR HELP

A few minutes later, a lady came in, and as soon as she entered, she turned her badge around but not before I saw the word psychiatric. I started crying uncontrollably, and she hurried over to me and tried to calm me down. Once I had calmed down as much as I could, she asked, "Why are you crying?"

I answered, "Everyone in my life has taken advantage of me," even her when she turned her badge around, so I couldn't see what type of doctor she was.

She immediately turned her badge back around, and as she started to stitch up my arm, she asked me questions about my life and what I had been through. As I was trying my best to tell her, my voice became very shaky. She proceeded to tell me that I was not crazy, just tired, and needed some rest. She recommended I go to the hospital for a few days, and when I said I didn't want to she explained that if I signed myself in then I could sign myself out, but if she signed me in then I wouldn't be able to leave until she said I was able to.

I agreed and signed the papers, and then called my kids' grandparents and told them what was going on. They told me to take the time I needed because the babies would be fine. Mr. Payne apologized for what had happened to me and said he would work to help me with the kids moving forward as much as possible since they were retired.

One of my cousins just happened to be at the hospital while I was there, and he asked me what was going on, but I wouldn't tell him because I didn't want Ozell to find out. She always felt she had a reputation to uphold and finding out that her daughter was in a mental facility after trying to commit suicide would not have set well with her.

After I got into the ambulance to go from the hospital to the mental facility, he got on the phone and called Ozell. She spent three days calling every facility until she found where I was.

After I checked in and got a change of clothing, since I didn't bring any, I cried for a couple of days straight. I cried so much my eyes swelled up until they looked like slits.

As I lay on my bed, I cried out to God, "Where are You? I need Your help!"

Then I really thought I was going crazy because I heard His voice with my own two ears. He said, "What do you need?"

I said, "I want someone to love me without trying to take advantage of me. Someone in the military I can travel with because I love men in uniform."

Maybe that was my issue; I was looking for love in a uniform. I told God I was tired, lonely, and just wanted to be genuinely loved. He told me He loved me and was going to take care of me. He also said that when I left the facility, I would go back to the same issues, but the difference was I wouldn't go back to the same me.

After spending a couple of days crying, my body was so exhausted that I hardly had any energy to get up, but I knew I had to. I got cleaned up and dressed and went to eat breakfast. I was starting to feel more relaxed, but that was just the calm before the Ozell storm hit. As I walked back from breakfast, the front desk told me I had a phone call, but the only people I thought knew about my situation were Mr. and Mrs. Payne, and I knew they wouldn't tell anyone.

I went to answer the phone, and it was my mother—Hurricane Ozell. She started our conversation with why I didn't call her and tell her where I was because when she found out she was embarrassed and seemed more concerned with what other people thought about my situation than what I was going through. She cussed me out and called me all sorts of names until I started crying all over again.

The person at the desk must have said something to my doctor because she came over, took the phone, and told Ozell I would not have any more phone calls. I could hear Ozell on the other end screaming about coming to get me out of there, to which the doctor said that if she came up there, she would not be let inside. They also told Ozell she was part of the reason I was in there in the first place. After that, the doctor hung up on her. My heart was beating so fast from fear of what would happen once I left that place.

FACING THE STORM

I spent the remainder of my time there not thinking about getting better but rather what would happen once I left. The only thing that kept me sane was hearing God's voice speak to me again, saying I was not going back alone. When the day came to leave, I didn't know how I was going to get home, but the front office said my ride was there. I didn't know who it was, so I slowly walked to the exit, and lo and behold, it was Ozell. I could have wet my pants out of sheer terror when I saw her. She came to me and said she was there to pick me up.

My heart was beating so fast because I just knew she was going to scream and cuss me out because other people in our family found out what happened "to her" because my cousin couldn't keep his big mouth shut. After we got in the car, I prepared myself for the onslaught of cuss words since no one was around to hear her, but she didn't do it. After she started the car, she turned to me, and I immediately flinched.

With tears in her eyes, she said, "I didn't know you were hurting that bad. I'm sorry for not helping you."

After we went inside, I told her I had to go to Mr. and Mrs. Payne's house to see my babies and take them home. After I hugged and kissed all over them, I took them home to my apartment, only to find out there was an eviction notice on the door. Even though I was sad to see it, I reminded myself I was no longer dealing with my issues alone because Jesus was with me.

Chapter Six
LOVE

WHO WILL LOVE ME?

I spent so much time looking for love yet gravitated toward the wrong people. I had to go back to that little girl who sat in the yard and just talked to God. This time, I wasn't alone because my babies were with me. I remember one night, while we were sitting in the living room of my apartment watching television, I stared at the two of them and felt guilt in my heart about what they went through even though they had no memory of it. So many tears streamed down my face that I couldn't see straight. When my two-year-old baby girl saw me, she got up off the floor, came and hugged me, and said, "Mommy better now?" You can't imagine what that did for me. I had never felt love like that before in my life.

I was at home one night, and Donita called and asked if I wanted to go to the club with them. Originally, I said no, but then something inside of me said I should go, so I called her back and said I would go. I only had twenty minutes to get dressed before they left, so I called their regular babysitter to come over and stay with them. I got dressed, kissed my babies (who were ignoring me by this time because they loved their sitter so much), and left with my sister and our friends.

It was Friday, October 18, 1984, and all I wanted to do was babysit purses, drink a soda, and sing to the music, but God had other plans. Back when I was in the mental hospital from a nervous breakdown a year after I got my babies back, I cried out to the Lord and He answered me back. I thought I was really going crazy. He asked me only one question, "What do you want?"

My answer was simple—I wanted to be loved. I wanted a husband, a father for my children who would love them as though they were his own, someone I could grow, build, and travel with. Well, I guess I got my answer because while I watched everyone dancing, I heard a voice say, "Do you want to dance?" The most wonderful feeling came over me. I then heard another voice that whispered, "This is your husband." I turned to see who was speaking in my ear, but to my surprise, there was no one there. Y'all, I fell in love with a voice before I saw the face.

I turned and looked to the other side and saw the most handsome face with a wide smile and gentle eyes. Without thinking, I said yes, and we proceeded to spend the rest of our time at the club together. After we danced to a few songs, we went back and sat with my group. They started throwing questions at him and asked if he wanted one of them, which took him by surprise, and I just laughed and said he was off limits. They sneered but quickly got over it.

I finally thought of asking him his name, which was Torrence, but everyone called him Trapp. After we finished dancing, I asked him which branch of the military he was in, to which he curiously asked me how I knew he was in the military. I said, "Only military would come to the club wearing a white t-shirt under their shirt," and he just laughed. I told him my brother was in the military before, and I also shared about my kids' father having been in it as well.

It was the beginning of a long night and life with this man. By the time the evening was over, we had both shared our life stories and phone numbers. For the first time in ages, I found myself relaxed and comfortable with who I was. I don't know why I shared myself with him, but it felt right. Maybe it was the Lord who whispered in my ear telling me Torrence was my husband. A new season is dawning for me. Trapp and I became friends first.

For my birthday, he came to my apartment to pick me up and asked if my children were home. I never allowed my children to meet someone right away, so I had them go over to Donita's house before he came to pick me up. I told him the reason why I was not ready for him to meet them, and he had no choice but to be okay with it. We went out to dinner and had a wonderful time, and he eventually brought me back home. And no, we were not physical. I had enough of those kinds of dates and wasn't looking to be anyone's one or two-night stand.

A NEW SEASON

Mr. Trappier and I became friends, but there was something so special about him. He was no knight in shining armor, but since the Lord said he would be my husband, I wanted to see where this relationship was headed. I can recall the moment I decided to let him meet my children. It was Thanksgiving, and since Ozell always cooked a big spread and everyone came to her house to celebrate, I invited Trapp to come over. Ozell's house felt like the safest place for them to meet him for the first time. My family members were all there, and if Gary didn't like him, I wouldn't continue to see him because he was a very good judge of character.

Ozell's house was a house full of relatives eating, dancing, and having a good time while listening to the loud music playing. The day celebration became a night party and moved outdoors to under the carport. It was getting late, so I decided it was time to take my babies home.

Trapp dropped us off at my apartment and returned to the military housing. The next morning, I got the babies ready to go to Mr. and Mrs. Payne's house for the weekend. As I sat in my apartment, Trapp called and asked if I wanted to spend some time with him. Since the kids were with their grandparents,

I said okay. He picked me up, and we spent the whole day together. And when we got back to my place, I knew he was truly going to be the one, but I kept it to myself.

As time passed, I invited him over one night to have dinner with the kids and myself. I wasn't a good cook back then, but I did my best to make a good meal. He came over, and after we sat down to eat, I formally introduced my children to him. He already knew that my son Johnny Jr. had special needs, so he wasn't surprised when he met him. We enjoyed dinner together, and afterward, the kids went and watched television while we talked about life.

There were many more dinners before he decided I was the one for him, and in the middle of it, life threw a curve ball when we least expected it. Lucky for me, I experienced a lot of them growing up, so I wasn't broken up when one came my way. Several months after we were together, he decided to move in with us. And around February of 1985, I came home from work and Trapp was sitting on the couch crying. I was nervous, wondering what had happened.

He told me the girl he had a one-night stand with before we met was pregnant with twins but wasn't sure if the babies were his or not. He asked me not to leave him, and I told him the only way I would leave him was if he didn't take care of his children if they were, in fact, his. We sent her some money for the babies each month, but then she started asking for more and more. I guess since he was in the military, she thought he was making a lot of money, but I was the one working two jobs because he wasn't able to due to going away on military assignments a lot.

After her last request for money for a motor in her car, I told him he had to get a DNA test for confirmation, and if they were his, then he would have to provide for them. I experienced my children's father abandoning his children, and if I were to stay with Trapp and they were his, then we both would ensure they were taken care of.

He got in touch with the babies' mother and prepared to take a DNA test, with him giving his blood on the West Coast, and she took the babies to give their DNA in South Carolina. Once the test confirmed what I already knew, the South Carolina Child Support Department sent him a letter acknowledging paternity and what his monthly support amount would be.

In addition to child support, I told Trapp he should also help with money for their birthday, Christmas, Easter, and summer clothing. I felt that since my children had him as a father full time, receiving everything they needed, we should help the twins' mother out as well. Once again, she started making irrational demands, which caused us to stop the extra money and send only what the courts required.

Life wasn't always a bed of roses, we had our ups and downs regarding finances, the kids on both sides and the pain of the past I was still trying to get free from. I know Trapp was trying his best to understand what I was going through, but I needed professional help to deal with things that kept creeping up in my heart.

HEALING ON THE WAY

In August of 1985, before we left for Texas, I joined a small church in Los Angeles because a friend of mine kept asking me to come with her. I kept saying I would but had no intention of going. After she asked me for the ninth time, something shook me on the inside, and I said yes (for real this time). That Sunday, I got up, got the kids dressed, and invited Trapp to go, but he was not interested, just as I had been a couple months prior. I said, "Okay," and left with the kids.

Church was good, and the praise and worship music was inspiring, but the message preached was hitting me in ways I had not felt in a very long time. After the message, the preacher did an alter call for salvation, and my legs were moving faster than my mind could comprehend. I found myself up front being prayed for. Before I knew it, I had received Jesus as my Lord and Savior, was slain in the Spirit, and began speaking in tongues.

This went on for an hour and a half, at which time they picked me up since I was only 110 pounds soaking wet and carried me into another room and allowed me to bask in the presence of the Lord. When I finished listening to God speak to me about a multitude of things, I got up refreshed and excited for this new life in Him. When I went home to tell Trapp, he was sitting on the sofa drinking a forty-ounce of Olde English 800 and watching the game. I was so happy about what happened to me that I couldn't stop talking about it. He just said, "Great, what's for dinner?"

I couldn't understand why he wasn't as excited as I was. I started attending regularly, just me and the kids, until one Sunday the pastor asked me about my life, and I told him. He and his wife asked me about my living situation, and I also told them about Trapp. They admonished me that, as a Christian, I should not be living out of wedlock with a man who was not my husband. So, after church service, I went home and told Trapp what was said and told him he had to move out until we got things right.

I also said if he was not going to be a Christian, then we had to separate. He thought I was crazy and said he had just moved out of his military housing and had no other place to go. I asked him to go to church with me just one time, and he didn't say anything. When the next Sunday came around, I didn't get up to go to church because I didn't want the pastors on my case. However, Trapp did get up, got dressed, and said he was going to go to church. I said, "If you are, you'll have to go alone."

Before I knew it, he was on his way to church. He sat through the service, and when the alter call was made, he too found himself up front for what he thought was just getting prayer. Little did he know God had other plans. The pastor laid hands on him and asked him to repeat the sinner's prayer, and Trapp received Jesus as his Lord and Savior.

When he got home, he was excited about what had happened, and I said, "Man, why didn't you go with me?" I knew that the Lord had to deal with him alone without any assistance from me. He had a friend who was not into the things of God at all, and when Trapp told him about getting saved, his friend tried to talk him out of it and go drink with him that evening. Trapp was not quite an alcoholic. He did drink a bit, but never to excess.

I never liked his friend because whether Trapp was a Christian or not, his friend was a womanizer, and I didn't like being around him. One time, his friend and girlfriend came over to our house to hang out, and they asked if we wanted to trade partners for one night. At first, we didn't understand what they meant but soon figured it out, turned down their invitation, and ended the night and the friendship.

BECOMING A FAMILY

One night, Trapp came home from work and threw several hundred dollars toward me and said, "Go and get wedding rings because I am being transferred to Texas, and I want you and the kids to go with me."

I had previously told him that if he ever got transferred to another location, I wouldn't go with him as his girlfriend because my children were my top priority. But as his wife, we would all follow him. I guess he understood the assignment. Little did he know that I had already seen a set of wedding rings at the jewelry store on the first floor of the building where I worked. I even tried on a set and told the jeweler I might be back to get them.

Trapp and I talked about what kind of wedding we would have, and he gave me a choice. He said, "We could spend all of our money and have a nice-sized wedding, or we could have a small wedding and use the rest to relocate to Texas and buy new furniture for our new home."

Since I am practical, I chose the latter. I focused on our future and not feeding people at a wedding. November 9, 1985, was the day my last name changed, and the old season ended, and a new one began. I was now Mrs. Torrence Trappier. The two of us went to a small chapel and got married and told my family afterward. Ozell was happy for us. I thought everyone would be angry since we did it alone, but they all welcomed him to the family. We all celebrated that night at Ozell's house.

February 1986 came, and it was time to leave California for Texas. I flew the kids out to their grandparents in Louisiana and returned to prepare for our move to Texas. Before we left, Trapp had one last short assignment he had to leave for. He had been gone for a couple of months while I was packing when the unthinkable happened. It was one of my last few days at my job, and my friend who rode in with me left her sneakers in my car. She asked for the keys so she could go and get them. When she came back in, she had this strange look on her face.

I asked her, "What happened?"

She said, "Your car is not there!"

I was in shock. I ran out of the building and stood where my car had been parked, but it was gone. I immediately ran back in and called the police, who came and took down all the information. They tried to check the cameras, but they were not working at the time. I was so devastated since that was the first car Trapp and I bought.

I loved that car and prayed that whoever took it would get caught. After Trapp got back from his assignment, I told him what happened. Even though he was angry about it, he said we could get another one once we made it to Texas. I left all my information with Donita, and I told the insurance company to get in touch with her or myself if the car was ever found.

We were finally off to Bergstrom Air Force Base on the outskirts of Austin, Texas. Three weeks after we left, Donita called to inform us that the car was found by a lady who had just moved into her place. She noticed it out back in the alley, but there were children playing in it. She assumed it was stolen, so she waited until nighttime and investigated. She saw my name and Donita's phone number on a piece of paper and called her to inform her of the missing car. Donita then called me, and I called the insurance company.

Torrence and I flew back to California to retrieve the car after the insurance company had it fixed and drove it back to Texas. I thought that would be the end, but no. After I drove over fifteen hundred miles through the hottest parts of the country, the car started to drive funny. It was slowing down and would not accelerate. I called Trapp, who called a tow truck, and after it was checked out, we found out that the car repair place that the insurance company used in California didn't check the fluids in the car, so the engine melted after driving it so far and for so long.

I loved living in Texas. It was different and very laid back, and after we bought a second car, I would drive through the countryside just to relax. The air was clean but hot and dry. After moving there, we found out we missed our cut off time for military base housing, so we had to rent a duplex in town for a short while until our name came up again. I was able to purchase new furniture before getting the kids from Louisiana. They loved our new spot and played freely outside as it was a safe place for them. My heart was able to relax as well.

THE CALL

A year after we moved to Texas, I was asleep when the phone rang. It was the time of the night when you know something is wrong, and you're afraid to answer but you do anyway. Well, it was Gary on the other end of the line.

He said, "You have to get back home as soon as possible."

As my heart began to race, I asked, "What's wrong?"

He said, "Ozell doesn't have much time left, and you need to get back as soon as possible."

I was perplexed because no one told me she was still sick with cancer. She told me she was in remission and that I needed to go ahead and move to Texas with Trapp because she was all right. My whole world began swirling until my knees buckled. I jumped up, told Trapp, and he made flight arrangements for me to head back home.

Thankfully, the kids were on their winter break from school and were with their grandparents in Louisiana, which was only a six-hour ride from where we were, so I knew they were already taken care of. I loved Trapp but still didn't trust anyone besides Mr. and Mrs. Payne with them, even though he never gave me any reason not to.

I flew back to California, and when I walked into Ozell's bedroom, she didn't even know me. She thought I was one of the nurses coming to care for her until she heard my voice. After being in there for a while, I asked them why no one told me she was still sick. They said Ozell didn't want me to know because she felt I was her weakest child at the time. I stayed there for ten days with the smell of cancer—an odor you can't describe to anyone.

While I was there, I prayed and said, "Lord, I can't watch her die, but I want to say goodbye."

As I sat in Ozell's bedroom, a social worker called, saying Judy had given birth to a baby girl six months prior but didn't tell anyone. The social worker said she had been trying to track Judy down because the foster family that had my niece was willing to adopt her if Judy or a family member didn't claim her in the next couple of weeks. In California, if the parent goes missing for six months, they terminate parental rights, allowing the adoptive parents to move forward with an adoption.

When Ozell got wind of this, she told them to bring her grandbaby home because she wasn't going to let anyone raise her grandchild except us. Everyone looked at Judy, and she acted like it was nothing to her. Judy's son Dexter was excited to have a little sister because until my niece Dana came along, she only had four boys. Judy was still deep into her drug addiction and didn't know how to take care of a little girl, so between Dexter doing his best to take care of his little sister and us enjoying a new baby in the house, Dana was in good hands. On January 25, 1989, Ozell finally succumbed to cancer. Two weeks after her funeral, Judy was murdered. Baby Dana went to stay with Donita who already had another one of Judy's sons since his birth.

ANOTHER ONE DOWN

That year was extremely hard for me, as well as the rest of my family, but in time, we made it through, not knowing we'd be facing tragedy again very soon. I remember flying in for a weeklong visit, and as I made it to Ozell's house, I was greeted by my remaining siblings. We decided we were going to have a family dinner the next day, so Donita went back to her apartment that evening, and Gary, myself, and a young lady he was seeing accompanied us to the street races.

We had a blast and were headed back to Ozell's house when I heard a still, small voice telling me to go back to Donita's house. I said, "Okay," but kept heading toward Ozell's with Gary and his lady friend. Then the voice said it again but louder, and again, I said, "Okay," but kept heading to the house with Gary. Then, the third time, it was so loud on the inside of me that it caused me to shake, and I said, "Okay, I hear you Lord," and then asked Gary to take me to Donita's house.

He dropped me off, and I spent the night at Donita's. We got up the next day and went to Ozell's house after going to the store to get the food to have a cookout when we were met by Albert stumbling off the porch steps like he had experienced some traumatic stressful event. I remember looking at his face while he was down on the ground. He turned his face long enough for me to see a grin on it, but it didn't look like him but rather someone or something else.

When he realized I caught him, he got up. My brother, Ricky, never saw the look on his face, but I did. From that moment on, I paid close attention to Albert. Once he got up, he said the police called, saying Gary's car was found seven blocks away in an alley, and there was a body in it that was set on fire. Once everyone came over, we told them what had happened. I even watched the news earlier that morning and saw the car and a body bag being pushed over to the coroner's van and said to myself that the family of the victim would be horrified to learn of their loved one dying like this, but in reality, it was us.

YOU'RE COVERED

My whole world came crashing down. I decided to sleep at Ozell's house the next night where I had a dream where I saw Jesus in the doorway of my dining room while I was sleeping in the living room on the sofa.

He said, "Darlene, rest for you are covered."

I said, "Yes, Lord. I know," and went back to sleep only to be awakened by a very loud noise.

When I woke up, all the lights were on, and the television and stereo were on at the highest volume. When my eyes were finally awake, I saw a group of young men in the living room. Then Albert came in wearing only white underwear and white socks. As I looked around, I counted fifteen of them. I yelled at him for being so disrespectful and to get those guys out so I could sleep. He turned to them and told them to leave me alone. I turned over and went back to sleep.

The next morning, I went and yelled at Albert for having so many people there while I was trying to sleep. He said there were only four guys, and I told him I had counted fifteen. He said I was lying and that's when I remembered what Jesus said to me in the dream. I couldn't believe my own flesh and blood brother would or could try and hurt or even terminate me. After that, I went back to Donita's place, told her what happened, and stayed with her until I left to go back home to Texas.

We had Gary's funeral, but my heart was so broken that my body felt like it was locked in place. I couldn't move. I even tried to remove my hand from the door handle of the hearse to go inside the church, but my fingers seemed glued to the door. My sister-in-law came and was able to help me inside, but I never looked at the casket. I sobbed the whole time and don't remember anything after that.

My one-week vacation turned into three so we could memorialize my brother. We had to have him cremated since he was not fit for viewing. Once the funeral was over, I went directly to the airport and flew home. I once again tried to put the pieces of my heart back together. Being away from California made it easier but not necessarily shorter. I revisited the old church where Trapp and I were saved to receive some spiritual guidance before returning home. That church was truly a God send, and every time I returned to California, I visited them.

Chapter Seven
WHOLENESS

UPS AND DOWNS

Until Trapp, my track record with men was not very good, and it got me thinking about my own father and why he wasn't in my life. There was this one night I was sitting in my bedroom thinking about where my father was through all the ups and downs I had endured. Gary was like a father to me in every way that mattered, but I still would have liked to have my biological father around to help me maneuver through life.

When I was seventeen, Donald, a cousin of my father, came to see Donita and said our father had been looking for us for many years. We hadn't seen our father since I was five, and now that he had found us, he wanted to get to know us. Donita wasn't interested in meeting him, but I was curious about who he was and what he looked like, and I had a lot of questions for him. Donald called my father on the phone, and I was able to speak briefly with him. He said that he was going to come and see us, but never did. After that, I believed everything Ozell had said about him and put him out of my mind.

After Ozell died, I began to think more about my father, and I started to search for him since Ozell made us promise not to look for him until after she died. She passed away on January 25, 1989, from breast cancer; my sister Judy was murdered on February 2, 1989; I lost a pregnancy in April 1989; my close cousin died from AIDS in May 1989; and Gary was murdered on August 3, 1990. With so many deaths, my heart ached for my father even more, especially after Gary was killed.

I started the search by remembering when my father's mother passed away and requested a copy of her death certificate. I knew someone would be listed as the informant along with their relationship to the decedent. I found one of my father's brother's names listed with an address and phone number and prayed he still lived there. I called the number and, lo and behold, he answered the phone.

I said, "I am Darlene, and I am looking for my father."

He said, "Your father had a major stroke right after he spoke with you all those years ago. I will reach out to him tomorrow and let him know you are looking for him."

I asked, "Can I get the number?"

He said, "I have company and can't do it tonight, but I will tomorrow."

He also told me about how he knew my mother and that she was a loose woman back in the day. He could have left that part out of the conversation and kept it strictly about my father. I guess he was not a fan of Ozell, but I didn't care because she had been saved, and after she passed on, I knew she was with the Lord.

The next day, he called with the phone number and said my father was expecting my call. After I hung up, I stared at the number to see if I was really looking to reach him. I picked up the phone and nervously dialed the number, and for a second, I thought about hanging up because if his brother had negative feelings about my mother then maybe my father would not want to talk to me. Before I could hang up, he answered.

"Hello" was all that I heard. I paused for just a quick second, and then there was another "Hello?"

I said, "Are you Donald Nelson, my father?"

He said, "What's your name?"

With a nervous voice, I answered, "Darlene Brown."

He asked, "Do you have a sister named Donita?"

I said, "Yes."

The next thing I heard on the phone was crying, and I didn't know how to react.

I asked him if he was alright, and he then said, "I have been searching for you guys for years."

My heart sank at first, but then it was as if the light went on inside my heart, and finally, with those few words, I felt wanted. We spent the next several hours talking about our lives and plans to finally meet in person for the first time in over thirty years. I knew he had other children—my half-brother and sister.

I called Donita and told her I found Donald, but she said Ozell had been her mother and father, and she didn't need to meet him. I told her that was not going to stop me from doing so. I knew she was just scared to open her heart to him. I decided to go and meet him and my siblings by myself for the first time without Trapp and the kids, just in case things didn't turn out as I hoped.

A WHOLE NEW SIDE OF THE FAMILY

I headed to Detroit, Michigan, for the first time in my life to see the other half of who I was, along with my little brother and sister who I vaguely remember from my childhood. All I could think about as I made my way to Donald's house was, *Lord, what do I call this man? Do I call him Donald, Dad, or what?* So many things were swirling around in my mind, but I had come that far and couldn't turn back.

I finally made it to his house, where he was waiting for me outside. Since he had a stroke, his voice was very slurred, and at times he struggled to form the right word. However, since my son had a speech problem, I was able to understand him. We hugged each other, laughed, cried, and he took out several photo albums with pictures of Donita and me in them.

He asked me about Ozell, and I told him she had passed away several years prior. Then he asked about Donita and my other sister Linda, which I found strange since we all thought Linda had a different father. He insisted Linda, Donita, and I were all his daughters. I was very surprised to hear that but told him Linda had also passed away and Donita was not ready to meet him yet. He was sad but understood.

I enjoyed my trip there, especially when I met my sister Teresa (Peaches) and my brother Cameron (Bingo) after decades of being a part. Peaches was so cute, and she had two of the most adorable children, Angel and Michael. It was nice having a younger sister since I was the youngest girl in my mother's house. As the week went on, Peaches and I spent a lot of time together, along with my dad and sometimes Bingo. We talked about our early lives and how much we all went through.

They lost their mother at a very young age, but Donald did not take them in afterward. They went to stay with one of their aunts until they reached an age where they were able to stretch their wings and go on their own. When I met Bingo, he looked like one of the members of the Five Heartbeats singing group. His hair was straightened, and he dressed very well. I guess all the women in Detroit were after him, but to me, he was my little brother.

After a couple of days, I was able to meet their side of the family. I was very nervous since their mother was the "other woman" in this triangle of children; however, my reservations dissipated after meeting them. They cooked a full spread for me when I went over to their aunt's house. I thought I would get a lot of questions about Ozell and maybe some nasty stares, but they were very kind and welcoming. I especially enjoyed being around their cousin Freda. She made me feel like I belonged and, to this day, treats me like a sister.

While I waited for my flight to take off, all I could think of was how I missed having them around in my formative years. I was also able to get a lot of questions answered from my father about what happened between him and Ozell. He acknowledged he made a lot of mistakes with other women, on top of living a life that wasn't the best for having children.

Even though I was happy to see him, I still felt hurt about some things I had endured as a child because he was not there to help me maneuver. I shared everything I went through, and he cried after realizing the choices he made back then affected our lives as well. He apologized a lot while I was there, so I started letting go of some of the hurt.

Once I made it back to my family in Texas, Peaches and I kept in regular communication through great phone calls. I told her I was coming back, but this time I would bring the kids. Trapp was going on military assignments, so he couldn't go. This was helping me feel better about myself because since Ozell had passed, I was a literal mess.

I spent the first year and a half trying to wrap my head around the fact that when she came to visit me in Texas, she gave her life to the Lord in my living room. Then two short years later, she was gone. I felt like I couldn't breathe, think, or reason at all. I thought I was having a nervous breakdown again. She always said I was her most sensitive child, and I was manifesting it with a couple more suicide attempts.

SILENT SCREAMS

Before I found my dad, I was screaming at the top of my existence, but no one could hear me. I was not able to focus enough to even cook a meal for my kids or wash a simple load of clothes without breaking down. I was also developing bad headaches, losing weight, and staying to myself. I didn't realize how bad it was until, one day, I was sitting in the living room of our home and my baby girl Tanisha came over to me and gave me a hug and said, "Mommy, it will get better."

I was so caught up in my own hurt that I didn't realize my babies were seeing my decline. Trapp tried to help me, but I couldn't focus on his voice long enough to understand what he was saying. Then one night, I was lying in my bed and heard a voice tell me to get up and go into the bathroom. I thought I was going crazy because I heard voices again. I got up quietly to not wake Trapp up and went into the bathroom.

The voice said, "You are needed and must get yourself together because the enemy wants to kill you. If you keep going in your current direction, your family will suffer the consequences of your actions."

I was crying but had my hand over my mouth so no sound could come out. It was the Lord God speaking to me, saying He was there to help me get through it, but I had to trust Him alone. I stayed in the bathroom for so long that the sun came up. I took my shower, got the kids up and ready for school, and the weight that was on my back literally lifted so much that I almost lost my balance when I stood up.

I didn't want to kill myself anymore, but it took some time for me to finally breathe, laugh, or run again. During this time, my family suffered tremendously because Trapp and I argued a lot. One early morning, I caught him over-disciplining my son, so I grabbed a knife and said if he put his hands on my child again, I would kill him. This whole situation almost caused us to call it quits, but God had something else in store. I didn't know that my family was now on the devil's radar, and his sights were set specifically on my special needs son.

JOHNNY JR.

My precious boy attended elementary school but was transported on the special needs' bus every day. His teacher was supposed to be there to receive him once he arrived. Sometimes, the bus would let him off alone without any supervision, and he walked right in with the other kids who were there waiting for the staff to arrive. The lights were usually off with only the janitor and kitchen staff working in the back.

One day, some boys around his age who were not special needs took notice of him arriving and decided to ask him to come and play with them. While he was twelve in age, mentally he was five or six. They told him to go into the bathroom to play, not knowing what awaited him were horrors beyond his understanding. They pushed him in, locked the door behind him, and one of the boys started beating him up. He screamed for me to come and help him. The same boy knocked him down, punched him in the face, and forced him to do things I can't even speak about. Afterward, they threatened him if he told me.

This went on for a couple of weeks, until one day, I got a call from the school asking, "Did you send Johnny to school with a bunch of money?"

I said, "No. I will talk to him when he comes home about it."

When Johnny Jr. got home, I sat him down and gently and calmly asked him, "Where did you get this money from?"

He said, "I took it from your wallet."

I asked, "Why did you take it?"

He said, "To pay a boy to not hurt me."

I got a little scared to ask him the next question but had to.

I asked, "How did he hurt you?"

He told me the whole story. My blood began to boil at hearing the details of what happened to someone who was so gentle and wouldn't hurt a fly. After hearing everything, I immediately called Trapp, the police, and then the school. The police came to the base where we were living and spoke with Johnny. When I contacted the school, they told me to bring him back up there to the place where he was assaulted. No way was I going to do that.

The police had me take him to the emergency room to get checked out. Thankfully, there was not any physical damage, but the psychological damage was done. With the help of detectives, we were able to identify the student, and he was removed from the school, but not after he had his friends punch my son in the face again. My son has the biggest heart and to know that someone took advantage of that made me want to commit the unthinkable. The police, my lawyer, and the therapist said that if I did what I wanted to, then Johnny would feel as if he was to blame if I went to jail.

When we filed charges against the boy, we found out the school knew of the abuse that the boy was going through from his father and grandfather but did nothing to protect him, my son, or any other child at that school. I believe Johnny was not the first, just the first who told. We also filed a lawsuit against the school, superintendent, and principal. I was grateful Johnny and Tanisha would no longer go to the school because we were now slated to move to New Jersey anyway. I took them both to their grandparents' house in Louisiana for a couple of months until we got situated in New Jersey.

While New Jersey was a fresh start, schools were no better for Johnny. The kids didn't abuse him in the same way, but they pushed him around in the hallway until I started taking him into the school and class myself. Tanisha went to school on base, so she was in a more secure situation, but Johnny's situation had my blood pressure going all the time.

We were finally able to get him registered at Burlington County Special Services School for special needs students, and I felt much better because I knew they would look out for him. He began smiling again, which was one of his greatest attributes because when he smiled, he could melt your heart like butter.

Just knowing my beautiful boy finally found a sense of peace caused my heart to relax. We were excited about the freshness of this relocation. I didn't yet know what was awaiting me personally here, but we, as a family, forged on together into new opportunities.

Chapter Eight

FAITHFULNESS

ADJUSTING TO NEW ENVIRONMENTS

We lived in McGuire Air Force Military Base housing on a nice, big cul-de-sac where other active-duty military families lived while their spouses were assigned there. It was quiet during the day, and when the kids came home, they all played together. After getting settled into our new home, I started looking for work. I did temporary work until I landed my first permanent job working as a medical claims adjuster for an insurance company.

The people there were nice, which allowed me to excel rapidly. I was unaware of the northeast union reputation, but I finally got an up-close introduction to it when I worked on a claim. Even though the end of the workday came, I was still working to finish it so I would not have to do it in the morning.

My union representative came over to me and asked, "What are you doing?"

I told her I was finishing the claim I was currently processing.

She said, "Since we are union workers, we cannot work past a certain time. You must clock out for the day."

She added that she understood I had never worked a union job, and if others saw me doing it, there would be trouble—not in the sense of physical harm but loud noises and complaints. Plus, management would start to demand more from the union staff. Even though I was at the end of the claim, I had to close it down and finish it the next day.

One weekend, the church we started going to had a softball game, and I was on second base. The guy running to it thought he could slide in but lost his footing and came down on my ankle—all 240 pounds of him. I ended up at the emergency room after trying to walk on it for the rest of the day to no avail and found out that it was, in fact, broken.

I was on crutches for church that Sunday, and when Monday came, my husband drove me to work, and I clocked in as usual. I went to my desk and propped my foot up on a crate so I could get to work. That was when the owner of the company came in and walked by me, saw the crutches, and asked me what had happened. I told him the story, and he said out loud, "This is what dedication looks like."

You could have heard a pin drop because I guess some of my co-workers thought I was showing them up, but all I wanted to do was my work. My department manager came over and commended me for coming in but said that I should have stayed home. After my husband picked me up from work, he said that since it was a long way going and coming, he could not take me anymore, so I had to stay home for two weeks. Well, that did not sit well with me because I was not a stay-at-home person. I have always enjoyed getting up, going to work, and being productive.

Over the next five years, I had three different jobs, not because I wasn't happy with them, but because the second job ended up relocating nine months after I started, the third one downsized and with low seniority, I was laid off. The first job called me and asked if I wanted to come back as a senior claim's adjudicator, and I said yes since it brought me closer to home.

Life was getting better until August 3, 1996. My precious babies' biological father, Johnny Sr., reunited with his biological mother, who then found out she had grandchildren and reached out to me to let them visit her in Florida. For two years, I said no, but then one year I said yes without going to the Lord to pave the way for their safety.

Trapp and I needed some time together. Since we had lost support from Mr. and Mrs. Payne due to their passing away, the kids did not have anywhere to go during the summer, so I said yes. I told her we were driving to South Carolina, and if she could meet us there, we would transfer the kids into her care for two months during the summer school break. I also told her I would make flight arrangements when it was time for them to come home, but she insisted on driving them back.

PROMISE KEEPER

I told her I wanted them to fly home and that I would contact her when the time came. I kissed them, and for some strange reason, I told Tanisha that if she got into trouble and could not reach us, then to call on Jesus. Little did I know that those words would truly be used. The time came for them to come home, so I called to let them know I was making airline arrangements only to be met with, "They left yesterday."

I was shocked that she would ignore what I said, especially since this was the first time she had visited with my children. I was angry but decided to go to the store and prepare a meal for when they arrived. After buying groceries and returning home, I checked the voicemails on my home phone and there was a message for me to call Nash General Hospital regarding my daughter Tanisha.

I did not think it was serious at the time, but when I reached the hospital, I was told, "You need to get here as soon as possible."

I could not process what the person was telling me, so I asked, "What is wrong?"

She said, "They were in a car accident, and Tanisha needs your consent for treatment."

I was sitting in shock in my living room, still unable to understand what was going on. I asked, "What happened to Tanisha?"

She said, "They were in a one-car accident, and Tanisha sustained the most injuries."

I asked, "What injuries did she incur?"

She answered, "A head injury."

I still could not process the severity of the situation. I gave my permission over the phone and told them I would be there as soon as possible. I hung up, called my friend Vanessa, and told her what happened. She and her husband came over, and when I saw Vanessa's face, the reality of the situation suddenly hit me, and I began to break down.

She grabbed me by both sides of my face and told me, "Now was not the time for that."

Trapp was on assignment in the field, and I could not reach him, so I had to deal with this by myself for the time being. My friend's husband made travel arrangements for me, and I changed my voicemail message to alert Trapp to call Vanessa when he made his daily call at 4:00 p.m.

I made it to the ticket desk, but there was a lengthy line. When you are a child of God and mother you forget about the fear aspect and become tunnel-visioned. I went past everyone and turned to all who were in line, and said, "My children were in a car accident, and the plane I need to get on is leaving in twenty minutes. Please let me go ahead of you."

I turned around to the ticket person, and she just pointed to the gate along with everyone else. I ran as fast as I could to meet the plane. Thankfully, the ticket person called upstairs and told them to hold the plane for me. I made it to Raleigh/Durham Airport, picked up my rental, and got on the road to the hospital, which was an hour away. On the way there all I could think about was how I was going to tear the kids' grandmother apart with my bare hands.

It was so quiet in the car that I could hear my heart beating. While I drove, I searched for something to listen to in my purse when I stumbled across an audio cassette and put it into the player. Now, was that not God for the only tape in my purse to be a message on forgiving the unforgivable?

I listened to that message all the way there, and when I finally made it to the hospital, my heart had changed. I went in, told them who I was, and that I was looking for my children. I found Johnny first walking down the hall with bandages on him like a mummy. I took him to the bathroom to remove the bandages so I could see what happened. To my surprise, he only had three cuts that required a couple of stitches. I walked back with him down the hall and told him to go to the waiting room until I checked on Tanisha. I had not seen his grandmother yet, so I kept my focus now on Tanisha.

After seeing that Johnny was okay, I was able to calm down a little bit. I walked into the ICU department past all the glass-walled rooms. I looked into each window to see if she was in there, but she was not. After I passed a few rooms, I was met by a young lady who asked me who I was looking for, and I told her I was Tanisha's mother. She turned and pointed to the room at the end of the hall in the corner. I headed toward it and was stopped by another woman, who said she needed to explain what was happening before I saw her, but I kept walking as she talked.

As we made it to Tanisha's room, the woman touched my shoulder and said, "Tanisha has been seriously injured, and they did not think she would make it through the night."

I began to blank out to the woman's voice. As I entered the room and walked over to look at Tanisha, my first impression was not fear but bewilderment because this person did not resemble my daughter at all. I turned and told the nurse, "This is not my daughter," but she assured me that she was.

They had to shave all her hair off. Her face was swollen beyond recognition. Her eyes were closed, so I could not see them. I began examining her from the top of her head to her feet. It was not until I saw her feet that I believed she was my daughter. She had Donita's feet, and she also had a braided bracelet on her ankle that she never took off. If it were not for her feet or the bracelet, I would have never believed it was my daughter.

FORGIVENESS

After spending what seemed like a lifetime with her, they told me she needed to rest and to check on my son again before I came back because the doctor was coming in a little while to talk to me about her condition. I reluctantly did so because I knew that now I had to deal with their grandmother who disobeyed my direct instructions concerning my children.

I left the ICU ward and walked down the hallway to the visitor's room, which seemed like it was a million miles away. I finally made it there and sat down in the nearest chair. My mind seemed like it was in another dimension because I could not hear anything or anyone. I stared into space, and when I looked up, I saw the kid's grandmother standing in the doorway of the waiting room.

When our eyes met, I could see she was extremely nervous and crying, but instead of thinking about how many ways I could kill her, my heart melted. She ran over to me, knelt, and said, "I'm sorry, I'm sorry."

I hugged her and said, "I forgive you," before I even thought about it.

Why did I say that? I told myself.

God knew that once I said something, I always held myself to it.

I said, "Now is not the time to deal with this because Tanisha needs us more."

I got up and went to the bathroom to have my breakdown. Staring into the mirror, I heard God's voice say to me, "How are you going to deal with this?"

I said, "What?"

He responded, "You have two ways you can deal with this situation—as her mother, and you will be burying her; or as her sister in Christ and prayer warrior, then she should come off that bed of affliction."

I stared into the mirror for a few more minutes then told the Lord, "I will fight as her prayer warrior."

It took me two days to pull myself out of my flesh. I said to the devil, "The battle is on."

I arrived at the hospital around 5:00 p.m., but Trapp did not get there until 10:00 p.m. that night because the military had to get him transportation from the woods in South Carolina. While I was waiting for Trapp, I went back to the ICU to speak with the doctor.

He said, "There is too much damage. You need to prepare to bring her body back home."

I responded with Psalm 118:17, which tells me, "She shall live and not die and will live to declare His wonderful works."

The doctor said, "You are in shock."

I said, "I am standing in faith until the Lord tells me to let go," but He never did.

THERE'S LIGHT DAWNING

Trapp, Donita, the kids' biological father, and my pastors at the time came in. Even my nephew Gary drove down since he was on the East Coast managing some business. The church we were members of started a prayer chain for her and us. We were there twenty-eight days, but on the twelfth day, she woke up at noon, which happened to be my son Johnny's birthday.

Trapp and I never left the hospital, and we all took turns going into her room to check on her. I tried to eat but my stomach could not hold anything, so I went the first couple of days without much sustenance. One morning, I went into her room to check on her and the nurses were standing at her door crying. My heart started to drop, but I quickly tried to compose myself.

I went into Tanisha's room, not knowing what to expect. I called her name, and she blinked. I looked at the nurses and realized why they were crying. They knew she was alive and awake. I thought I was dreaming, so I turned to her and asked her to open her eyes again, and she did, but this time I leaned over to her, got right in her face, and said, "I see those beautiful brown eyes of yours."

VISION IS CLEAR

I turned and threw my purse to the side. Then I ran out of her room, out of the ICU, and down the hall, yelling, "She's awake!"

Everyone was crying as I passed them. I then realized I had run all the way to the hospital exit door yelling. I quickly turned back around and ran back to the ICU and into her room. I gently kissed her on her forehead and waited for the doctor to come in and give us an update. Trapp and I both listened to him, and he said that he did not understand how she was still alive since her injuries were so severe. I told him I knew.

He said he was not a believer in God, but her recovery was supernatural. Since she was going to make it through, they were going to prepare her for facial reconstructive surgery since ninety-eight percent of her face was fractured. The day came for her facial surgery, which we were told was going to be several hours long. Forty-five minutes after the surgery was scheduled to start, the doctor came out to meet with us.

I was confused and asked, "What happened?"

He said, "I don't understand what has happened. When I had another x-ray taken of her face for us to map out our plan, it showed her face had healed completely as if it had been two months."

It had only been two weeks!

He said, "I only had to put a plate under and over her left eye, and none of her facial bones had shifted out of place."

I winked at him and gave him a big Celie from *The Color Purple* smile.

TRANSITION

Despite her miraculous facial recovery, we were told Tanisha would be paralyzed on her right side, blind, permanently brain damaged, and never have a period again; thus, she would never have children. We were also given a list of nursing homes because, according to them, she was going to require too much care for us to handle.

We had her medevacked to a rehabilitation hospital in Philadelphia and were told by the staff there that she was not going to wake up from her post coma state for three months, yet she was walking with a quad cane after three weeks. She had a setback though when one of her feet started to develop dropsy, but she came home from the rehab hospital after forty-five days and went back to school for the second half of the ninth grade. For the remainder of her high school years, she was placed in special needs classes.

She experienced bullying, but I immediately stopped that, and she graduated from high school with honors and went to community college but majored in socializing. After her high school graduation, we asked Tanisha what she wanted for her graduation, and she said that she wanted to go to Walt Disney World®. We took her and had a wonderful time.

Chapter Nine

LIGHT HAS ENTERED THE ROOM

NEVER TURNING BACK

Life can test even the strongest relationships, and ours was no exception. But God can and will see us through it all if we will give Him the chance. After my son's assault in Texas, and our subsequent relocation to New Jersey, Johnny Jr and I had to fly back on separate trips for the court hearing and lawsuit regarding the boy who assaulted him. When we arrived at the court hearing, we walked right by the boy and his grandmother. I paused for a quick second right in front of him, but my lawyer told me not to engage because it could affect the outcome. So, I pushed all my emotions to the bottom of my soul and kept walking.

The judge decided the boy was to be given community service and non-forced counseling. I wanted to call my relatives back in Los Angeles and have the boy disappear, but I could not do it, especially after hearing he had been assaulted by his father and grandfather for over two years. I felt like I was betraying my son, who was still suffering from the aftereffects of the trauma.

How could I have empathy for someone who hurt my precious son so violently and yet support my child in the process? There was only one way—Jesus. The school system decided to settle out of court after my son had his deposition, and when we left Texas, we shook it off and never looked back at that place again.

Between Johnny Jr's situation and Tanisha's car accident, I had nothing left to give and no one to lean on to get me through it all. The church we had joined in New Jersey was a small one and grew over time. When we first visited, I told Trapp it was not the place for us, and when we did find one, we would talk about it and join as a family. However, when we went there for a second visit, they asked if people wanted to join, and Trapp stood up. This left me sitting there, and since I didn't want him to look stupid, I stood up as well.

When we made it home, I told him I felt uncomfortable and that if anything happened because of his decision, it would fall on his shoulders. Little did I know how those words would ring true. After being there six years, the pastor (who had a reputation for preying upon women in a weakened state) decided to take advantage of the pain I was in to initiate an affair with me. My husband was sent to Desert Storm, my son was having a nervous breakdown, my daughter was coming home from the rehab hospital after the car accident, and I was having a miscarriage.

I felt like I was going over a cliff with no one to help pull me back. That was when things began to spiral out of control. I lived in a fog for a couple of months, until one day, I was sitting on my back deck at home and began to wake up from what appeared to be a long sleep. I began to panic because I could not understand how I got there or how I was going to get out of this compromising situation with the pastor.

There were many times I wanted to tell my husband about it when he returned home, but fear kept me locked up in emotional chains. I told the pastor that what had happened was wrong and it needed to be told, but he said it could not. By the time I finally got up the nerve and decided to tell Trapp, the pastor had told his wife a lie, and when we all met, I was being treated like a Jezebel rather than the victim in the situation. Trapp told them he was leaving and taking his family away from that church, but we still had a lot to sort out between us.

MOVING FORWARD

We ended up going to another church, and we told them the unvarnished truth about why we left the other church. I immediately began taking classes to repair my foundation while Trapp did the same through the Sunday morning and Tuesday night services. We both eventually joined various aspects of the church and began to flourish.

Johnny Jr and Tanisha also received healing in the areas that they needed while in children's church. The church we left also went through some changes, with the biggest one being that the members all left, and therefore, they had to close their doors and relocate. The new church provided much needed healing and repair of Trapp's and my relationship. Through the teaching of the Word of God and fellowshipping with other believers, we were on our way.

After seven years there, God instructed us to step out in faith and finally start our own church, based on the word that was spoken over us twenty-five years prior at Victory Christian Center in Round Rock, Texas, via Pastor Billy Joe Daugherty. The church started to grow, and people were delivered and set free.

We opened a dollar store near where we lived, and it was thriving. The community was happy with the name we chose for it: My Dollarstore. We wanted the community to feel like they had a place of their own. Through the store, we were able to begin our unnamed outreach ministry by helping people with free food when they needed it, clothing donated to us by the cleaners that had closed its doors, and donated furniture we placed in the warehouse for families that needed it.

Everything was going well until the terrorist attacks of September 11, 2001 hit, and the economy went on a downward spiral. We then made the decision to close the store at the end of our lease agreement. This was hard for me because I had left my corporate job for this and now closing what gave me a reason to get up every day. I enjoyed the interactions with everyone who came in and helping families get back up on their feet. Children were bringing me their report cards, and if they did good, they got several treats, but even if they did not, they still got treats along with words of encouragement.

After closing the store, Trapp said I could keep it going from our garage (the helping people part). My Dollarstore gave people dignity and a sense of purpose each day. We would have the same group of people come in there four or five times a day, sometimes just to talk and other times to talk and shop. I did not mind it at all, and my kids had a place that helped them with their people skills while also being in a safe environment.

RELAPSE

Just when we thought we were out of the woods with Johnny Jr, he began relapsing from the trauma in Texas. Money was missing from the cash register. He ran away from home and even set a fire in our basement. The fire department came and put it out, but when we went to court, the judge gave me a choice of Johnny going to jail or to a court assigned facility since Trapp was away again.

They felt as if I could not take care of him on my own, especially with Tanisha still recovering, which took a few years. I chose the facility for special needs adults. It was the hardest thing I ever had to do. He was my firstborn, and I could not help him at all. All I could do was stand there while two ladies from the facility took him from the courthouse, put him in a white van, and drove off.

My son, my beautiful son. I felt like I failed him all over again. I could not see him for the first thirty days, so they could get him acclimated to this unfamiliar environment. When I found out I could see him, I was up there as often as they would let me. He was angry with me at first for making him go, but three years later, he was glad. He knew I could not give him the help he needed. His smile, which I had not seen for over six years, finally returned, and he was upright and no longer hanging down low.

As for the person who started all of this in motion back in Texas, he got into some more trouble and ended up in prison for quite a few years. That made Johnny feel like justice was finally served. I had mixed emotions because the young boy had been abused but never received any help and only grew angry and bitter at the world. I know this because I found him on social media shortly after he was released and said a prayer for him.

Three years did not fly by, but eventually, Johnny was able to come home and start a new beginning. He got a job and dated a little bit, but mostly wanted to be back home with his family, and we were ready for him to come, too.

The choices I made in my younger years to have children by a married man, whether he was separated or not, started the chain of events that opened the door to the enemy to bring attack after attack. I felt like Job in the Bible, who went through a lot by losing his children, his wealth, and lastly, his health, but he never gave up. I have had some mountain highs and as many valley lows, but as I continued this journey of discovering who my Father really is and who I am, I began to place myself on the straight away.

NOT THE END, JUST THE BEGINNING

In December 2020, I almost died from COVID. While I was in the hospital for a month, I had no one else to rely on except Jesus, and I utilized that avenue as much as I could. I talked to Him, and He bathed me in His love through music, sounds of rainfalls, audio Scripture reading, and peaceful quietness. I took time to begin reflecting on my life and all I had been through, and I said to myself, *If I survived all of that, how could I let COVID take me out?*

The battle was on because I had people depending on me to make it through. I lost my hair; my skin was peeling; I was losing body fluid faster than the IV could replace it; my glucose levels went way up; my blood pressure went down a lot. I developed thrush down my throat, and the skin on my left arm looked like a bad case of psoriasis. I had body aches and a headache and lost twenty-five pounds, which I have since found again. I digress.

I was able to go home on Christmas Eve but had to quarantine in my own home for an additional ten days, but on January 9, 2021, my entire world came crashing down. While I was recovering at home, I received a phone call that caused my vocal cords to become arrested, then they acted like a caged bird that had just set free and soared as far as they could. My scream was so loud that my family thought it was one of the televisions in the house turned up high until they kept hearing me say, "No, Rose!" repeatedly.

My mind could not comprehend what I was being told because I was suffering from COVID brain, which was one of the long COVID side effects. The room was spinning like a fast Ferris wheel. My brain felt like it was about to tilt, and my body, which was already extremely weak, would not respond to any of my commands, so I just fell.

My sister, my best friend, Donita, had a catastrophic brain aneurysm and passed away the next day. I thought someone had just cut off my oxygen, and my brain was suffocating, and I could not process anything or anyone.

I asked God, "Why did You save me only to take Donita?"

He told me it was so I could finish the work He had for me to do. I did not want to finish it; I just wanted my sister back.

I spent the next ten days laying in pain while trying to get stronger so I could fly to California for her funeral, but I knew that even though my heart and mind were ready, my body still needed healing and rest.

I kept asking myself and God, "Why did I have to get sick at such a time as this when my family was in so much pain?"

I also asked God why He waited until I was at my lowest for her to leave me. I also asked Donita why she waited until then to leave me as well. I remember being on a video call with her for the first time ever two days before she passed away, and I kept looking at every detail of her face, her hair, and her clothing not knowing that the Lord was letting me etch her into my memory. I can still see her face as if I am looking right at her now.

Donita was hurt over things Rose had done to cause a rift between her and her granddaughter. She said she would never forgive her, and I kept telling her she needed to let go of all that anger because it cannot enter heaven. I told her to forgive her and let it go for the sake of her peace and mental healing. We spent two and a half hours on the phone, and I prayed for her before we ended the call, not knowing I was never going to hear her voice on earth again.

Two days later, she suffered an aneurysm, which encompassed most of her brain, and she did not recover from it. I asked the Lord to heal her, and He said He did, but it was not going to be in the way I was asking. For a split second, I felt nothing but peace. My tears immediately dried up as if I knew what He was saying was final and accepted the outcome.

This had never happened to me before, but now it did, and I was okay with it. I called her children at the hospital, and they put the phone up to her ear. I told her I understood and was ready to let her go, and if she was ready, then she could go home. I was operating without thought or negotiating with myself. I began to accept the things I could not change, believe in the things I did not want to and prepare for what was to come. She was the one I was the closest to and the only sibling I was not able to be at their funeral in person for. I could only participate by video because of my continued recovery.

While we were waiting the two days it took for Donita to fully transition, I had a phone conversation with my sister Rose, who was the only sibling capable of handling the funeral preparations. She was in so much pain that it caused her to become vile with statements of unwillingness to participate, that she and I never had a real relationship anyway, and to forget her phone number. I told her okay and hung up. From my bedroom quarantine, along with her eldest son Donte and my two cousins, we completed all the arrangements while Donita's other two sons and daughter were at the hospital until she passed.

I was able to see her transition via video call. I prayed over her and them before she completed her transition from earth to heaven, and a couple of hours later, I was staring at her earth suit, knowing she was no longer taking up residence within it. I had bittersweet feelings about it. On the one hand, I did not want to let her go, and on the other hand, I wanted her to be at peace. The latter won out.

The day came for the funeral, and it was a beautiful event with everyone laughing and some crying. Rose sat in the audience and did not once go up to say a word about her. It was okay because she was going through her own struggles. I kept and continue to keep Rose in my prayers to this day.

After Donita passed, I felt alone again for the first time in decades. I had assumed she would always be there and we would grow old together, but she went home to heaven before me. I was angry, jealous, and longed to be with her, but I knew that her family, as well as mine, needed one of us here. Since it was me, I had to fight to get my physical as well as spiritual self together.

CONCLUSION

IT WAS NECESSARY!

As I sit here and go over where I started out and my tumultuous beginning in life, through trials, tests, attacks, and temptations, I can see that the trials are what help us develop and become stronger, or we will succumb to them and not make it out. As a small child, life looked vastly different from today. All I did was get up, get dressed, eat, go to school, and play. Now I am the one doing the getting up and going to work every day, so my granddaughter and the rest of the family have a better life than I did.

People always compliment me on my smile and say that my laugh is contagious, but that was not always the case. There were times when I felt like the ugly duckling with a gap in my front teeth, a very thin body frame, bad acne from excessively oily skin, and a dark skin tone, which back then was not considered desirable. But today, I look at myself with all my extra attributes and say, "I am the most beautiful person on the planet."

As I grew in God, I started to understand and see that He made me beautiful, and just like Celie from *The Color Purple*, my smile grew, my self-esteem soared, and I saw myself as the most beautiful person in the world. I know I said it earlier, but I just wanted to say it again. Life still held some more trials, but I have and am still learning that no matter what is thrown at me I know I will rise back up again.

Jesus reminded me of that the day I gave my life to Him. My heart had to go through those seasons in order to be on the straight path I am now. No more mountain highs and valley lows, just the straight away. My children are now adults. Johnny has matured into the man of God the Lord told me he would. Tanisha is the mother to a beautiful daughter despite being told motherhood would never happen. I had COVID and was told I might not make it, but I am still here. Johnny was told he would not make it past what he went through, but he flourished. My husband and I are in an incredibly good place despite the attacks against us individually and as a married couple.

We started an outreach ministry called Beacon of Hope Inc. that helps individuals and families struggling through life's difficulties and challenges. We are also pastors of a church called New Beginnings Christian Center. These names were not by chance but by divine choice because everyone deserves a new beginning and a beacon to lead them to hope, just as we did.

I started out with wide-eyed dreams of being a lawyer, but then life tried to imprison me, sentence me to capital punishment, and destroy any hopes of freedom. But today, I am free because my heavenly advocate paid the price, removed my death sentence, and wrote my name down so that I can never be sentenced to eternal death.

ABOUT THE AUTHOR

Darlene Trappier grew up in Los Angeles, California, and was homeless at the age of nineteen with her five-week-old infant son. Her mother evicted her after Darlene took her own welfare check and refused to give her mother the money.

She told the Lord that if given the strength to overcome the seasons of pain she was facing, then she would return the same to as many people as possible. God has delivered her from the pain and helped her overcome her seasons of struggles. Darlene kept her word to the Lord by founding and operating a non-profit, faith-based organization (Beacon of Hope Inc.), which assists others who have struggled through life and just need a helping heart as she did. Her children work there with her.

Darlene now uses her life experience to help others overcome the pain of their past and move into the destiny God has for them. She has taken everything she has been through and views it as preparation for the ministry God has for her. Darlene is living the best season of her life today with her best friend and husband, Trapp.

darlenebtrappier.com
beaconofhopeinc.com
Facebook: Darlene B. Trappier
Instagram: Darlene B. Trappier

ENDNOTES

1) Fleming, Victor, director. *The Wizard of Oz*. Metro-Goldwyn-Mayer, Warner, 1939.

2) Spielberg, Steven, director. *The Color Purple*. Warner Bros, 1985.

Made in the USA
Columbia, SC
16 September 2024

41756941R00083